MOPED
MAINTENANCE &
REPAIR

CH

MOPED
MAINTENANCE & REPAIR
MORRIS FRASER

TAB BOOKS Inc.
Blue Ridge Summit, PA 17214

FIRST EDITION

FIRST PRINTING

Library of Congress Cataloging in Publication Data

Fraser, Morris, 1942-
    Moped maintenance and repair.

    Includes index.
    1. Mopeds—Maintenance and repair. 2. Title.
TL444.F73   1985   629.28′772   85-7973
ISBN 0-8306-1847-3 (pbk.)

DEC '85

Contents

Introduction

Of all motor-driven vehicles, the moped is probably the easiest to operate and the easiest to repair. Imagine a weekend mechanic trying to change a tire on an automobile. It is a fairly simple task, but one which could frustrate the mechanic and require a considerable amount of strength. Changing a tire or fixing a flat on a moped, however, is so simple that it often can be accomplished with no more than a wrench and a screwdriver.

Mopeds are for those who don't want to be concerned about the reliability or expense of their vehicle. They want to get on it and go. Nevertheless, any vehicle requires some maintenance and occasional repair.

Professional mechanics must charge a relatively large sum for their time and expertise in repairing a moped. To many mopedders, the expense is not worth it: they would rather do it themselves, save time and money, and learn something about their machine in the bargain.

Few books on the market supply a well-rounded knowledge of what a moped is, how it is operated, and essential yet easy repairs. This book should fill a gap in a mechanic's library and help moped riders better understand their vehicles.

Chapter 1

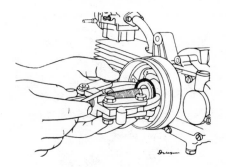

Learning About Your Moped

The motorized bicycle has been popular in Europe since gasoline prices increased there after World War II. The popularity of this single-person, low-horsepower, economical means of transportation grew to such proportions that today an estimated 25 million are on the roads around the world, with more than half of those in Western Europe.

The *moped* (MOtor-PEDal) originally had a limited number of fans in the United States. Before 1973, about 55,000 were being ridden, but the rapid increase in oil prices during the late 1970s spurred the moped's popularity. Today it is estimated that more than one million mopeds are ridden throughout America.

To date, 44 states and the District of Columbia have made the moped a separate category from bicycles and motorcycles, although to many law enforcement agencies it still is considered a bicycle. Most states have enacted laws on mopeds since 1970, when Michigan was the only state with special definitions about mopeds.

The specific limitations on speed and power vary, but all states agree on the basics: a moped is a two- or three-wheeled vehicle for one passenger, with a small, 50-cc. engine and helper pedals, capable of no more than 35 miles an hour, with a headlight, taillight, rear view mirror, and reflectors (Fig. 1-1). It has an automatic transmission (to avoid the intricacies of shifting), but it may be one-speed or two-speed. Thus, while there is no shifting, a two-speed

1

Fig. 1-1. The handlebars support virtually all of the operating controls.

transmission is capable of climbing steeper hills and providing a quicker getaway from a standing start.

Although the moped engine originally was designed to help the rider pedal, that function has been reversed, and the pedals are used primarily for starting the engine and for helping the engine overcome standing starts and hills. Another advantage is in case a moped runs out of gas; the rider can pedal the 100-pound machine to the nearest gas station—a strenuous lesson in fuel-watching that seldom bears repeating.

Most mopeds sold in the United States today have a number of extras that make riding more pleasant. A speedometer/odometer (Fig. 1-2) lets the rider keep to the speed limit on residential streets and tells him how far he has travelled. Front forks help absorb bumps in the road, and shock absorbers often are added to the rear wheel to smooth out the ride. Better models have a longer, motorcycle like seat for comfort on the increasingly longer rides mopedders are taking (Fig. 1-3). A tire pump and special tools generally are included when a new moped is purchased.

Besides the items a manufacturer supplies, dealers carry a wide range of accessories, from turn signals operated from the engine, to enclosed saddle bags for carrying extra equipment. An enthusiastic mopedder could increase by 50 percent the cost of his

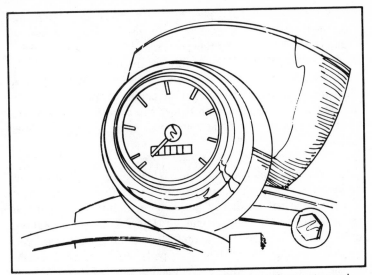

Fig. 1-2. The speedometer/odometer notes distances and current speed.

moped by hanging enough extra equipment on his machine. The decision to do so obviously is limited by what the mopedder wants to spend and the realization that the extra equipment means extra weight.

HOW THE CONTROLS WORK

The moped is designed to be simple to operate. If a person can balance on a bicycle, he can balance on a moped. If he is used to

Fig. 1-3. A long, motorcycle style bench seat makes long trips more comfortable and even may accommodate a passenger.

3

the braking levers on a ten-speed bicycle, he has only to learn how to use the throttle to be a mopedder. As with any machine, however, some knowledge of operation is necessary, and with a little practice most mopedders become skillful in the basic functions.

All mopeds have a switch, generally located on the handlebars, which allows the electrical parts of the engine to operate (Fig. 1-4). The switch must be turned on before the engine can be started. When that is accomplished, the engine may be started in one of three ways:

- Mount the moped and pedal. When speed is built up (about 5 miles an hour is enough), pull the clutch lever (Fig. 1-5), generally located on the left handlebar, just long enough for the engine to start—a second or two is often enough. The clutch engages and the engine starts. Turn the throttle on the right handlebar toward you and stop pedaling. Although most mopeds easily start in this fashion, the French Motobecane is designed to start more easily from a standing position, and other mopeds can be started similarly.

- Place the moped on its center stand. Position the pedal on the same side of the moped as you are standing, slightly above parallel to the ground. Grasp both handgrips for balance, squeeze the clutch lever, and place the foot nearest the moped on the pedal. Put

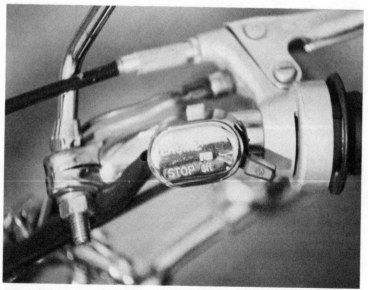

Fig. 1-4. The ignition switch connects the electrical system to allow the engine to start.

Fig. 1-5. The clutch lever engages the engine and lets the operator start the moped at a standstill.

most of the weight on the pedal. As it descends, the engine will engage. Turn the throttle slightly, being careful not to let the rear wheel come in contact with the ground and push the moped off the center stand.

● The final method of starting doesn't even require a pedal. You can begin rolling the moped down even a slight hill, build speed up to about 5 miles an hour, engage the clutch, and turn the throttle slightly. This is the easiest method of starting, although it does require the proximity of a hill. The second method often is the most popular way to start a moped.

Most motorcyclists keep their headlights on, even during the day, in order to give motorists additional warning that a vulnerable two-wheel vehicle is nearby. Safety-conscious mopedders, without even the extra power to force themselves out of trouble in a dangerous situation, have adopted the same procedure. A headlight switch may be located on the handlebar or on the headlight case itself. Most mopedders simply turn on the switch and never bother with it again (Fig. 1-6).

Having learned to start his moped, a rider next must know how to stop. Mopeds are equipped with both front and rear brakes, activated by hand levers on the handlebars (Fig. 1-7), in the same fash-

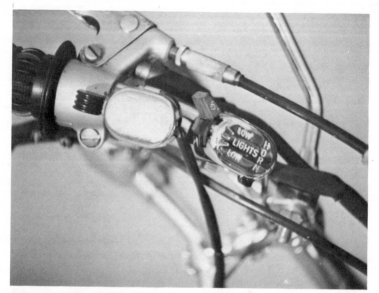

Fig. 1-6. The light switch operates the headlight; the horn button on the same control operates a buzzer-type horn; the switch at left controls turn signals as automobile turn signals are operated.

ion that a ten-speed bicycle's brakes are operated. For those used to the position of a ten-speed bike's levers, however, most moped levers are reversed. Thus, the left hand controls the rear brake, and the right hand controls the front brake. When stopping, the moped-

Fig. 1-7. Hand brakes on each handlebar provide maximum stopping power.

der must be careful always to apply the rear brake first. That stabilizes the moped and sets the stopping weight back to the rear. Then the front brake, which contains most of the stopping power, can be applied smoothly.

Mopedders should practice this maneuver until it becomes automatic—rear brake, then front brake. This is for a good reason; in a panic stop, applying the front brake first (or applying only the front brake) will cause the moped to stop short. The rider will lose balance and control and most probably fly over the handlebars and into an injury.

Handlebars are where a mopedder's hands will spend 95 percent of their time. Therefore, the handlebars should be located in the place most comfortable for the rider (Fig. 1-8). Handlebars can be adjusted forward and back. A rider should adjust them until they are comfortable, so that arms don't get tired from having to extend beyond their normal reach, and so that the bars are not so close to the body that control of the front wheel is reduced. The

Fig. 1-8. Arms should be comfortably extended to the hand grips when the rider is sitting almost upright.

handlebars and the rider's weight control the direction of the moped—if the handlebars are properly located, steering is made that much easier.

A horn button is located on the handlebars, often in connection with the headlight switch. The horn provides some warning, but most moped horns are soft and do not carry very far. They are more a buzzer than a true horn, but they do provide enough warning that at least pedestrians can get out of the way. Position the switch, if possible, on the handlebars in such a way that a finger or thumb of the left hand can activate it quickly (Fig. 1-6). Try to avoid using the right hand for anything other than controlling the throttle and applying the right-hand brake.

Adjusting the rear view mirror or mirrors often is a matter of personal taste, but the mirror should be angled to enable the moped-der to see as much of the road as possible to the rear and on both sides of the moped (Fig. 1-9). This often means sitting on the moped with both wheels on the ground, getting a reference point behind the moped, and adjusting the mirror until the rider can see the reference point (a car bumper, bush, or similar low structure) and know how close it is to the moped. All rear view mirrors, on mopeds, motorcycles, and cars, have a blind spot just behind the vehicle that the rider cannot see. A mopedder should be cautious in his use of the rear view mirror and, when turning or changing lanes, turn his head to either side to check traffic directly.

Fig. 1-9. Rearview mirrors on each side give the rider a better idea of the traffic behind him.

Fig. 1-10. Besides reducing the noise level, the moped muffler system is used to keep the vehicle within legal speed limits.

MOPED SPEED AND POWER

State laws vary on the maximum speed a moped may reach. Hawaii allows 35 miles an hour, the remainder have selected speeds ranging from 20 to 30 miles an hour, and Maryland has not set a speed limit.

Engine power may be 1-horsepower, 1 1/2-horsepower or 2-horsepower, depending on the state. While 21 states allow 2-horsepower, 13 other states permit 1 1/2-horsepower. The remainder of the states either limit to 1-horsepower or do not state a limit. Obviously, the less horsepower a moped has, the slower its top speed will be, but other parts of the machine can determine speed.

The simplest way to limit power is by attaching an exhaust system that will not allow exhaust gases to escape easily, pushing them back toward the engine and slowing it down (Fig. 1-10). Other ways to restrict power include the size of the sprocket the drive chain moves around—the larger the sprocket, the more power but less speed is transferred to the rear (drive) wheel; weight, which is a minor factor in determining speed—the heavier a machine (and its load) are, the slower it will travel; and tuning—an engine properly tuned gets the most out of the available power, but shims in the engine help decrease the speed at which it operates.

The carburetor jet allows air into the carburetor to mix with the gasoline/oil mixture and permit combustion. A larger jet will admit more air and create a better explosion, but the range of sizes of jets for the 50-cc. engine is limited enough so that the largest provides only a moderate increase in power.

The mopedder also must realize that atmospheric conditions contribute to a moped's power—a heavier, cooler atmosphere means more air into the carburetor. Cold air is not as efficient as cool air, so, depending on the size of the carburetor jet, a temperature of about 50 to 60° F will produce the best power. Adjustments have to be made over the course of a year in the moped's jets, because temperatures are not constant throughout the year or even throughout a given day.

Proper tuneups (see Chapter 8) and regular maintenance will assure the rider of the best possible consistent power from his moped.

STATE LAWS

Mopeds are regulated only by state laws. No single federal law governs all mopeds, thus it is possible to ride a moped legally in Colorado, where a 2-horsepower engine is legal, and not be able to ride legally in Ohio, where only 1-horsepower is legal. Similarly, a moped legally capable of traveling 30 miles an hour in Oklahoma would have to be adjusted before crossing the state line into Texas, where the maximum legal speed is 20 miles an hour. See Table 1-1.

Age limits of riders vary from state to state. Most states specify a range from 14 to 16 years-of-age for a moped rider, but South Carolina allows 12-year-olds to ride, and Arkansas and Oklahoma do not set a minimum age. Most states require a rider to be 16 in order to make sure that requirements of a driver's license are met (Virginia has a 16-year-old minimum age, but does not require a license). Some offer an optional moped license, and Texas requires a license for motor-assisted bicycles of everyone 15 and older. Some states will allow a moped to be ridden by anyone of the correct age with a learner's permit.

Most states require some form of registration, ranging in cost from Florida's one-time $5 charge to Illinois' $12 annual fee. Most states are in the range of $5 per year to $5 for a three-year registration. Many states are not strict in enforcing that registration, however, placing mopeds in the same category as bicycles and treating them accordingly. Because license plates are not required, states use registration as a means of locating and identifying stolen bicycles and mopeds.

Although speed and power limitations have been discussed, it may be pointed out that Maryland does not set a maximum speed limit, and two states (Nevada and New York) do not set an engine size or horsepower limit.

Insurance is mandatory only in five states, but most of the rest demand some sort of financial responsibility; if a moped rider causes an accident, he must show that he can afford to pay for repairs to another vehicle or for medical bills if someone is injured. Often, that takes the form of automobile insurance with a clause including mopeds, or homeowners insurance that includes such vehicles as mopeds and bicycles.

Motorcycle helmet laws have been enacted in several states. Such laws are controversial and occasionally have been repealed. Only four states require helmets for mopedders, and two of those have conditions that limit required helmets.

The term *moped* is an informal one. Most often, state regulations refer to them as motorized bicycles, but they also are legally defined in some states as "pedal bicycle with helper motor" (Arizona), "motorized pedalcycle" (Illinois and Pennsylvania) and, in six states that don't regulate mopeds (plus New York), they are considered motorcycles. Many states, however, are beginning to define the vehicle as a "moped," and the term seems firmly implanted in common language and appears to be gaining ground in legal terminology as well.

With the term "bicycle" attached to the moped, most law enforcement agencies do not separate mopeds from nonmotorized bicycles. Their accident reports generally note "bicycle," occasionally "motorized bicycle." A few local police departments are sufficiently concerned about the increase in moped use that they are attempting to break out the moped into its own category. Often, that involves consultation with state authorities, who use the designation quoted in state law.

Mopedders in a given community may be able to find an interested policeman who will make an effort within his department to note the difference and stress an educational program, with the mopedder's help, for the police and the community. It is important for mopedders to gain the cooperation of law enforcement authorities. Many still consider mopeds a small motorcycle and treat them as such. In those instances, mopedders should become familiar with state law in their own state.

Table 1-1. State Moped Laws (as of 1981).

STATE	AGE LIMIT	LICENSE REQUIRED?	REGISTRATION	*POWER/SIZE	MAXIMUM SPEED LIMIT
ARIZONA	16	yes	$8/year	1.5 hp	25
ARKANSAS	no	no	no	2 hp	30
CALIFORNIA	15 1/2	yes	$5 once	2 hp	30
COLORADO	16	yes	$5/3 years	2 hp	30
CONNECTICUT	16	yes	no	2 hp	30
DELAWARE	16	yes	$5/3 years	1.5, 55 cc	25
DIST. OF COL.	16	yes	$6/year	1.5 hp	25
FLORIDA	15	yes	$5 once	1.5 (no limit)	25
GEORGIA	15	yes	no	2	30
HAWAII	15	yes	$3/year	1.5	35
ILLINOIS	16	yes	$12/year	2 hp	30
INDIANA	15	no	no	1.5 hp	25
IOWA	14	yes	$5/year	no hp limit	25
KANSAS	14	yes	$5/year	2 hp	30
KENTUCKY	16	yes	no	2	30
LOUISIANA	15	yes	no	2 hp	25
MAINE	16	yes	$5/year	2 hp	30
MARYLAND	16	yes	no	1.5	none
MASSACHUSETTS	16	yes	$3/2 years	1.5	25
MICHIGAN	15	yes	$5/year	1.5 hp	25
MINNESOTA	15	yes	$3/year	2 hp	30
MISSOURI	16	yes	no	2 hp	30
MONTANA	16	yes	no	2 hp	30
NEBRASKA	14	yes	no	2 hp	30
NEVADA	16	yes	no	no hp limit / no size limit	30

STATE					
NEW HAMPSHIRE	16	yes	$3/year	2 hp	30
NEW JERSEY	15	yes	no	1.5 hp	25
NEW MEXICO	13	yes	no	no hp limit	25
NEW YORK					
Class B	16	yes	$5/year	no hp limit	30
Class C	16	yes	$5/year	no size limit	20
N. CAROLINA	16	no	no	no size limit	20
N. DAKOTA	14	no	no	no hp limit	30
OHIO	14	yes	no	2 hp	20
OKLAHOMA	none	no	$6/year	1 hp	30
OREGON	16	yes	$6/2 years	2 hp	30
PENNSYLVANIA	16	yes	$6/year	no hp limit	25
RHODE ISLAND	16	yes	$10/year	1.5 hp	25
S. CAROLINA	12	no	no	1.5 hp	20
S. DAKOTA	14	yes	no	2 hp	30
TENNESSEE	14	yes	$10.50/year	no hp limit	30
TEXAS	15	yes	$6/year	60 cc	20
VERMONT	16	yes	$10/year	2 hp	30
VIRGINIA	16	no	no	1 hp	20
WASHINGTON	16	yes	$3/year	2 hp	30
W. VIRGINIA	16	yes	$8/year	2 hp	30
WISCONSIN	16	yes	$5/year	no hp limit	30
WYOMING	16	yes	no	2 hp	30

*-engine size 50 cc unless otherwise stated.

For instance, in Colorado the law governing mopeds leans heavily on regulations concerning bicycles. According to state law, a moped rider must have a driver's license, which is subject to points accumulated for traffic violations. If a moped rider is involved in an accident, he can be arrested, charged, and even sent to jail, but no points can be assessed against his driver's license under the moped regulations. That is particularly important when a mopedder drives a car as well and where driving privileges can be suspended with enough points on the license.

Police are often unaware of the peculiar rule regarding mopeds, however, and attempt to place points on the rider's license. It may take a court appearance to resolve the matter, but the concerned mopedder will make every effort to educate police concerning such a rule.

Again, state laws vary as to where a mopedder may ride. Taking Colorado again as an example, a moped may, with few exceptions, go anywhere a bicycle may go (Fig. 1-11). That means designated bike ways, within 400 feet of an automobile road bed, are open to mopeds. Certain cities, however, can restrict access to off-road bikepaths through city parks, for instance. Bicycles, and

Fig. 1-11. Off-road bike paths in many places are designed for moped operation as well as for bicycles and runners, but local laws vary considerably.

Fig. 1-12. Repair of mopeds often just means taking a tool and applying it to the appropriate part. With the right knowledge and a little common sense, repairing a moped is no more difficult than doing a little fix-up around the house.

thus mopeds, are not allowed on certain portions of the Interstate highway system but, generally, a moped can be operated on residential streets, throughways, and major roads, regardless of traffic volume. It should be observed, however, that the right to ride on a heavily traveled street does not mean taking up space in the center of a 40-mile-an-hour rush-hour lane. It may be legal, but it is foolhardy.

Riding a moped safely and knowledgeably is a major part of keeping it in good condition, but even the best-maintained machine needs special care once in a while. Parts wear, tires go flat, and dirt, oil, and grease envelop chains, hubs and engine parts.

A mopedder buys his moped in large part because of the savings in gasoline and repairs. It follows, therefore, that he should be interested in knowing as much about maintenance and repairs as possible in order to save money. Moped repairmen generally are competent, but they must charge a good price for relatively minor work that anyone with enough skill to change a light bulb should be able to do (Fig. 1-12).

Learning about the equipment on the moped, how to take it apart, repair it, and reassemble it will pay dividends to the mopedder who wants to save money and who, on a long trip, breaks down and must repair his machine on the spot.

Chapter 2

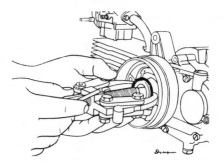

Troubleshooting

A moped is a complicated piece of machinery compared to a little red wagon, but it is a simple piece of machinery compared to an automobile. Thus, while there are intricate parts that you may prefer to let a qualified repairman deal with, there are other parts that you can understand and, when necessary, adjust and repair at little or no cost. When you work on your own machine, you will have the satisfaction of learning more about the moped and of putting that knowledge to immediate and practical use.

Part of that learning stems from determining what is wrong with the moped when it does malfunction. That is called *troubleshooting,* and it involves detective work no less engaging than that in which James Bond engages—although explosions and pretty girls probably will not be a part of your investigation.

Troubleshooting is an art and not an exact science. Even expert mechanics may fail to locate the source of a problem, at which time they will sit back, scratch their heads, and review all the symptoms that caused the owner to hand over his machine to them.

In a basic sense, troubleshooting is determining that something is wrong, deducing why it is wrong, locating the problem, and solving the problem. Most troubleshooting can be done with a minimum of dismantling and a maximum of thinking. That means a thorough knowledge of the way the moped acts under normal conditions; the moped rider who intends to troubleshoot must be aware of anything out of the ordinary, and he can't do that if he doesn't know what the ordinary is.

As a simple example of troubleshooting, consider what happens when the headlight goes out (Fig. 2-1). The astute troubleshooter knows that the drive chain probably is not at fault, and the engine and clutch assembly have little to do with the operation of the headlight. The troubleshooter narrows his thinking to the electrical system: the rear lights probably aren't involved; the magneto seems to be all right because the engine starts. The search is narrowed to the headlight assembly: a wire may be loose, or the headlight switch may be defective, but those are rare occurrences. It is most probable that the lamp is burned out. So, whether the troubleshooter consciously goes through all these steps or not, he eliminates the least probable and ends up with the most probable solution—replace the lamp.

When you are troubleshooting, break down the areas of concern into logical units—the engine (Fig. 2-2), drivetrain, (Fig. 2-3), fuel system (Fig. 2-4), electrical system (Fig. 2-5), and frame and auxiliary items (Fig. 2-6).

ENGINE

The heart of the moped is the engine. If it doesn't work, the moped is not going to move very far or very fast. Thus, it is ad-

Fig. 2-1. The headlight draws most of the electrical current in a moped and is one indispensable item for safety.

Fig. 2-2. The engine is central to efficient operation.

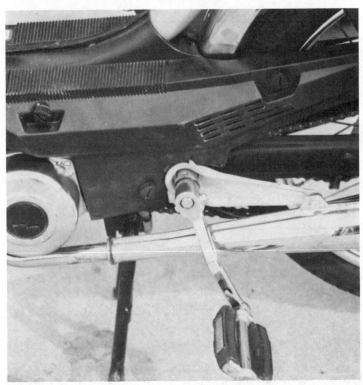

Fig. 2-3. Pedals are connected to the drive chain and to the bicycle chain.

19

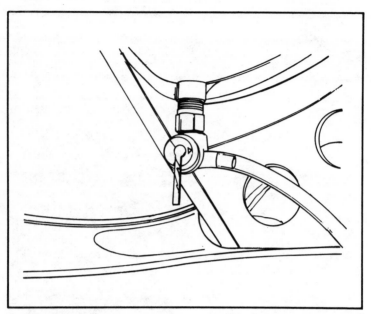

Fig. 2-4. Fuel supply is controlled by a simple yet vital gas cock located underneath the gas tank.

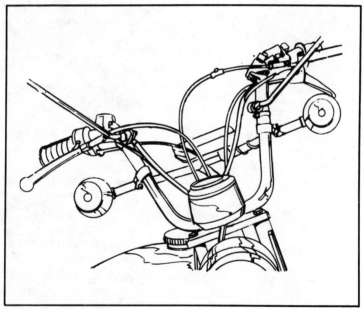

Fig. 2-5. Starting with the many wires around the handlebars, the electrical system runs throughout the moped.

Fig. 2-6. Proper operation of the front fork assembly means a smooth, enjoyable, and most of all a safe ride.

visable to concentrate on the engine when symptoms indicate. The engine is directly or indirectly related to all other parts of the moped, so we may consider other segments of the machine while troubleshooting the engine. See Table 2-1 for symptoms and possible cures.

Table 2-1. Engine Troubleshooting Chart.

SYMPTOM	POSSIBLE CAUSE	SOLUTION
Engine won't start.	No gas.	Fill tank.
	Plugged fuel line.	Clear with compressed air or rod.
	Bad spark plug.	Check or replace.
	Spark wire bad.	Replace.
	Fuel cock closed.	Open to let gas through fuel line.
	Cold engine.	Use choke to let gas into carburetor.
	Switch is off.	Turn it on.
	Timing is off.	Check and adjust contact points.
Engine runs rough.	Timing is off.	Check contact points, adjust or replace.
	Carburetor misadjusted.	Adjust carburetor.
	Vacuum leak.	Tighten all carburetor fittings.
	Plugged muffler.	Clean exhaust and muffler system.
Engine has no power.	Dirty or misadjusted carburetor.	Clean and adjust carburetor.
	Dirty air filter.	Clean or replace.
	Bad spark plug.	Clean, gap, or replace.
	Dirty engine.	Decarbonize cylinder and piston.
	Worn piston rings.	Replace.
	Chain is loose.	Adjust or replace.
	Drive belt worn or loose.	Adjust or replace.
Engine sputters or misfires.	Bad spark plug.	Clean or replace.
	Bad spark wire.	Replace.
	Poor gas-oil mix.	Drain; install new mix.
	Clogged air filter.	Clean.
Engine noises, backfiring.	Poor ignition timing.	Adjust timing.
	Carbon buildup on piston.	Decarbonize engine.
	Bad fuel.	Drain; replace.
	Loose crankshaft, clutch assembly, piston.	Adjust or replace.
	Broken or loose mounting bracket.	Repair or replace.
	Magneto rotor out of balance.	Replace.
Piston seizes.	Broken piston rings.	Replace.
	Too little oil.	Add oil, including squirting some into cylinder.
Clutch slips.	Oil on linings.	Wipe linings dry.
	Bad pressure plate spring.	Replace.
	Broken shoe return springs.	Replace.
	Idle set high.	Adjust engine idle.
	Cable too tight.	Adjust at handlebar.

DRIVETRAIN

The drivetrain includes the chain, rear wheel assembly and, for this purpose, the brakes. If something is wrong in this area, the ride will be harsh, or the moped may buck or provide a mushy or uneven ride. The brakes may grab, or—worse—not work at all. In all of this, concentrate for safety on the drive chain and the brakes. See Table 2-2.

FUEL SYSTEM

As under the section on engine troubleshooting, the fuel system could result in symptoms that seem to lead to other parts of the moped. Keep good, clean gasoline in the tank. Watch for condensation of water if the moped has not been driven for a long time, and be sure the oil is measured properly and mixed well with the gasoline. See Table 2-3 for troubleshooting fuel systems.

ELECTRICAL SYSTEM

The electrical system provides the spark—literally—for the moped engine to run. It also provides power, from the engine and

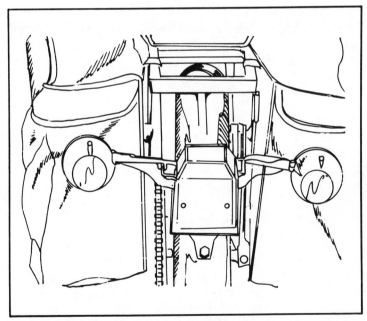

Fig. 2-7. It's easy to forget the rear light assembly, especially when hidden from a rider's view by saddle bags.

Table 2-2. Drivetrain Trouble Chart.

SYMPTOM	POSSIBLE CAUSE	SOLUTION
Lack of power.	Chain is slipping.	Adjust or replace chain.
	Underinflated rear tire.	Add correct air pressure.
	Brakes too tight.	Loosen brake cables.
	Axles not in place.	Set axles in proper position, with nuts and washers correctly tightened.
	Chain too tight.	Loosen chain.
	Chain worn.	Replace chain.
Brakes don't operate.	Cables worn or broken.	Check, adjust, or replace.
	Brake pads worn.	Replace pads.
Brakes grab.	Oil on linings.	Replace linings or sand slightly after wiping.
	Drums out of round.	Replace.
	Brake shoes glazed.	Replace.
Brakes stick.	Weak return springs.	Replace.
	Dry pivot cams.	Lubricate.
	Cable broken or dry.	Lubricate or replace.
	Cable stretched.	Adjust or replace.

magneto, to operate the lighting system and turn signals (Fig. 2-7). The first thing to check when an electrical problem is suspected is that all the bulbs are in good condition and that the wiring is in good condition and anchored securely. To troubleshoot the electrical system, study Table 2-4.

Table 2-3. Fuel Systems Troubleshooting Chart.

SYMPTOM	POSSIBLE CAUSE	SOLUTION
Engine stops.	Out of gas.	Add gas-oil mix.
	Fuel cock off.	Set cock to correct position.
Engine sputters.	Bad gas-oil mix.	Drain and replace.
Poor gas mileage.	Incorrect carburetor adjustment.	Set carburetor.
	Timing bad.	Adjust timing; adjust or replace points.
	Leak in fuel line.	Locate and patch or replace line.
	Leak in gas tank.	Drain gas, locate, and repair leak, or replace tank.

Table 2-4. Electrical Troubleshooting Chart.

SYMPTOM	POSSIBLE CAUSE	SOLUTION
Light doesn't work.	Broken or worn bulb.	Replace.
	Contact worn.	Resolder contact or replace bulb.
	Wire broken.	Replace or solder and wrap with electrical tape.
	Connection loose.	Tighten.
	Magneto not working.	Repair or replace.
	Wire shorting out.	Wrap bare spot with electrical tape or replace wire.
Light flickers.	Contact worn.	Resolder contact on bulb or adjust contact on unit.
	Loose wire.	Tighten connections.
	Bulb wrong size.	Use correct size bulb.
	Switch is bad.	Repair or replace.
Horn doesn't work.	Loose wiring.	Tighten connections.
	Worn wiring.	Wrap worn spot or replace wire.
	Bad switch.	Repair or replace.
Turn signal erratic.	One bulb burned out.	Replace bad bulb.
	Switch corroded.	Clean contacts.
	Battery weak.	Run moped for a few miles with headlight off to recharge.
Turn signal doesn't work.	Wiring loose.	Tighten connections.
	More than one bulb out.	Replace all bad bulbs.
	Battery defective.	Replace.
	Wiring to magneto loose.	Tighten connections.
	Ground wire loose.	Tighten connections.
	Switch bad.	Replace switch.

Table 2-5. Frame Troubleshooting Chart.

SYMPTOM	POSSIBLE CAUSE	SOLUTION
Wheel wobbles.	Loose axle nuts.	Tighten nuts.
	Bent rim.	Adjust spokes or replace rim.
Hard to steer.	Handlebars loose.	Tighten frame bolts.
	Tire pressure low.	Add correct air pressure.
	Bent frame.	Straighten frame.
	Bent forks.	Straighten or replace.
	Chain too tight.	Adjust chain.
Seating uncomfortable.	Seat height bad.	Adjust seat height.
	Seat bolt loose.	Tighten bolt.
	Padding worn.	Replace seat.
Ride bumpy.	Shock absorbers worn.	Replace shocks.
	High tire pressure.	Reduce air pressure.
Fatigue on long rides.	Handlebars misadjusted.	Set bars to comfortable position.

FRAME AND AUXILIARY ITEMS

If the moped has not been in an accident or gone over extremely rough terrain, the frame should remain in top condition as long as you ride it. When you go over curbs too sharply, however, you could damage the suspension. When you ride, get the feel of whether you are steering in a straight line. If it seems like you have to constantly overcorrect, or that the front fork assembly seems out of line with the rest of the machine, suspect a damaged frame or suspension. See Table 2-5 for possible cures.

Chapter 3

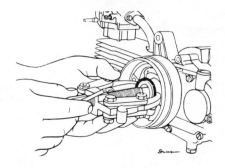

Preventive Maintenance

As a rule, a moped requires so little care (except at major intervals) and generally runs so well all the time that it is easy to forget that it is no different than any other piece of machinery. Preventive maintenance keeps little problems from becoming big problems and stops little problems from developing at all.

Much of preventive maintenance is routine. If you remember the proper gas-oil mixture, you will check it automatically as you fill your gas tank (Fig. 3-1). Regular checks of tire pressure will keep problems from developing, and you may even spot a slow leak in an innertube that could become a major problem should it blow on the road. Even regular checks of the spark plug will help continue good gas mileage.

Some things, however, seem to slip by the average mopedder. Because the chain always runs in an oval-shaped path, and because it always seems to pull the moped along just fine, some people forget that it requires care, too. Because mopeds have automatic transmissions, and there is no shifting (except in two-speed models, and even that requires no conscious effort), the transmission oil can be easily overlooked.

Mopeds, like any other machinery, run best at peak efficiency. People who complain about their mopeds not running right probably are those who don't continually check the simple things. Conversely, mopedders who seem to have no problems at all haven't found the perfect moped—they simply take a few minutes to regularly

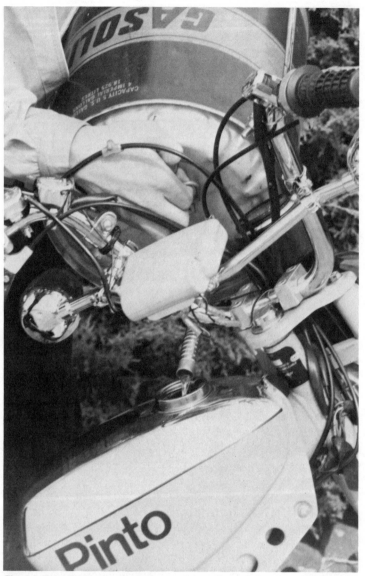

Fig. 3-1. The proper gas-oil mixture can be easily made in a 2- or 5-gallon container, ready for use at home.

check a few items that mean the difference between a safe, enjoyable ride and a bucking, spitting, coughing monster that fights the rider constantly.

OIL-GAS MIXTURE

From 1 to 4 ounces of oil is recommended for a moped's two-stroke engine. Regular engine oil can be used in an emergency, but two-stroke oil is designed for the special properties of a moped engine and should be used regularly.

Your owner's manual or a sticker on the moped will tell you just how much oil is recommended, but even that may not be a clear indication of how much you should use. Four ounces might be fine, but then again it might foul your spark plug if your engine doesn't burn that oil efficiently.

Even competent moped repairmen and riders disagree on how much oil should be used. The decision stems from whether they are more concerned with protecting the engine or with keeping the spark plug tip clean. More oil certainly will protect the engine well, but unburned oil will cause more frequent fouling of the plug. Less oil will help keep the plug clean, but damage to the engine is more likely.

From the standpoint of repair costs, it is simpler and less expensive to replace a spark plug than it is to replace an engine. The correct amount of oil mixed in the gasoline in the first place will keep the engine clean and free from damage and still not excessively foul the plug (Fig. 3-2).

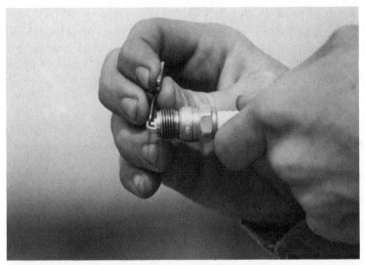

Fig. 3-2. A clean, properly gapped spark plug means better performance and better mileage.

Each moped, or at least each engine, is different. You can experiment with your moped and find the least amount of oil you can use that will effectively operate your machine. Start with the manufacturer's recommendation and each gas tank or so use half an ounce less oil if your plug seems to foul. You can trace fouling by noting any dark brown buildup around the firing end of the plug. Of course, if you see oil dripping off the plug when you remove it, you have another clue that too much oil has been used. Continue using less oil until the plug seems clean, with only light brown deposits around the firing tip.

Some riders insist on no more than 1 1/2 ounces of two-stroke oil per gallon of gasoline (an ounce per normal fill-up of eight-tenths of a gallon). Again, the amount will depend on your moped engine.

TRANSMISSION OIL

Just as with a car's transmission, the oil in a moped transmission keeps the moving parts from rubbing and wearing out and provides a certain amount of pressure to allow proper operation (Fig. 3-3). Dirt and engine emissions gradually build up in the oil, and the oil itself breaks down over a period of time and needs to be replaced.

The oil needs to be checked for proper level regularly and replaced on a regular basis. This is easy.

Most mopeds have a readily accessible filler hole that also serves as the filler for adding oil. Place the moped on a level surface, on the kickstand, and unscrew the filler bolt. The oil should be just below the level of the hole. If you can't see well into the oil pan,

Fig. 3-3. Among the lubricants used on a moped are (from left) two-stroke engine oil, cable lubricant, carburetor cleaner and transmission fluid.

Fig. 3-4. A used butter container will hold drained transmission oil.

slip a small screwdriver into the hole and measure the length of oily blade.

If the oil needs replacing (we come to the messy part), drain the oil. Slip a small container under the drain plug under the engine (a soft-spread butter container works nicely). Loosen the drain plug with a wrench, but remove it with your fingers (Fig. 3-4). Don't let the plug fall into the container; it's messier trying to retrieve it than it is to let some of the oil drain onto your hand.

Let the oil drain completely; do other tasks while you are waiting to make sure all the oil is drained. When the drip becomes occasional, move the oil-filled container carefully to one side and replace the drain plug. Tighten it with a wrench, but don't overtighten. That will make it easier to remove next time. The idea is to tighten the plug enough so that the oil won't leak out.

Use a small funnel (Fig. 3-5) to pour new oil into the filler hole. Check frequently so that you won't overfill. Replace the filler hole screw and wipe the area clean. Dispose of the old oil.

Each make of engine requires different oil, from Type F automatic transmission fluid to 30-weight engine oil. Use the proper weight for your engine.

LUBRICATION POINTS

Mopeds have few lubrication or grease points (Fig. 3-6). One

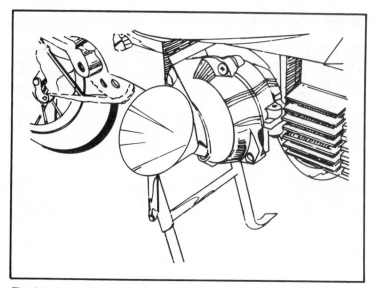

Fig. 3-5. A funnel makes it easy to add new transmission oil.

grease fitting may be found on some speedometer fittings at the front wheel (Fig. 3-7). Other than that, a drop or two of lubricating oil into the headframe of the handlebar unit and perhaps on the hubs (if they have oiling points) is all that is required from this standpoint.

Fig. 3-6. Lubricant can be applied to cable lubricating points on the handlebars.

Fig. 3-7. Apply lubrication to grease fittings at wheel hub.

At all times, however, if you feel a dry rubbing between two points on the moped, a drop of oil certainly won't hurt.

CHAIN LUBRICATION AND ADJUSTMENT

More people forget to lubricate their chains than they forget any other part of preventive maintenance. Lubricant dries up on a chain as easily as it does elsewhere, and a dry chain will wear itself and the drive sprockets quickly.

Lubrication is simple. Use chain lubricant (Fig. 3-8) and simply drip or spray the lubricant on the chain as you rotate it by hand with a pedal. Make sure the chain is thoroughly lubricated, but don't overdo it.

The messy part of lubricating a chain is immediately after you set down the can of lubricant. Rotate the pedal fairly rapidly. Extra oil will fly off, either onto you or the rear rim. Despite a little mess, thorough lubrication is vital on the chains.

Don't forget the bicycle chain on the right side of the machine (Fig. 3-9). It doesn't get the wear that the drive chain does, but it can stand some lubrication.

Light machine oil can be used on the chains in place of the special lubricating oil, but you will need to lubricate more frequently.

At the same time you lube chains, take the opportunity to ad-

Fig. 3-8. Apply chain lubricant to the drive chain, turning it easily.

just the tension on the chains. Loosen the axle nuts on both sides of the rear wheel (usually a 19-mm nut). Then tighten the expansion bolt nuts on either side (Fig. 3-10), making sure you turn the nuts the same amount on each side. Then retighten the axle nuts.

Always check your wheel alignment after adjusting chain ten-

Fig. 3-9. Make sure the bicycle chain is lubricated and adjusted.

Fig. 3-10. Extender bolts on each side of the rear wheel keep the chain at the proper tension.

sion. Spin the wheel and check for any small wobble that will throw you off balance and wear your tire out quickly.

Warning. Make sure the axle nuts are *tight*! Nothing can be more dangerous than a wheel slipping loose because you didn't tighten an axle nut.

The expansion bolts serve to take up stretch in the chain. Once you have reached the forward end of the bolt, it is time to take a link out of the chain and readjust the settings or replace the chain.

A link remover can be purchased or you can do the same job with a screwdriver and hammer. Prize out the master link, remove it, and then take out an extra link. Replace the master link and reassemble the chain around the sprockets to make sure it is of proper fit. Sometimes two links may have to be removed. Don't force a tight chain onto the sprockets; it will just wear out faster.

When checking tension on the drive chain, rotate the pedal and press on several points on the chain, always on the top side and as near the center as possible. With no one on the moped, you should have about a 1/2-inch of play in the chain. Don't overtighten. A rider sitting on a moped automatically tightens the chain. Too loose an adjustment will cause difficulty in riding and add wear to the chain; it could come off the sprockets, as well.

Tightening the drive chain will automatically adjust the pedal chain. That chain probably never will need replacement. With care, you might only replace a drive chain once during the life of a moped. (For cable lubrication and adjustment, see Chapter 5).

TIRE PRESSURE

Tires operate best at a specific pressure. Too little air pressure means a mushy ride and loss of steering control. Too much air pressure means a harsh ride and faster-wearing tires (Fig. 3-11).

Use the tire pressure specifically recommended by the moped manufacturer or stamped on the tire. Generally, you will inflate your front tire to 4 to 6 pounds less than the rear tire (even though the tires themselves are interchangeable). You might want to add a pound or two to the recommended pressure if it will increase your stability, but don't overinflate more than that (Fig. 3-12).

Rear tires wear out faster than front tires because they do more work. This can work to your advantage because you can get more life from your tires by rotating them. Wait until the rear tire has about half as much tread as the front tire, and then switch them (see Chapter 4 for procedures in removing tires). By the time the new rear tire wears out, the front should be ready for replacement as well.

Original-equipment tires often will last 10,000 to 15,000 miles, but rarely over that. Replacement tires, particularly radial designs, should last even longer. Few mopeds have been ridden more than 30,000 miles without major overhauls.

Fig. 3-11. Check air pressure in both tires regularly.

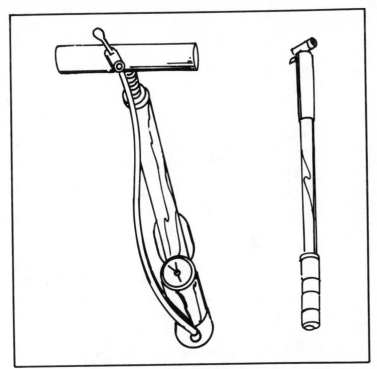

Fig. 3-12. Two types of tire pumps. The smaller one fits easily onto the moped, but does not deliver as much pressure per stroke.

SPARK PLUG GAPPING AND CLEANING

Spark plugs supply the fire that ignites the gas-oil mixture that comes out of the carburetor. The spark is made by sending an electric current from the point of the plug to the L-shaped metal prong at the extreme end (Fig. 3-2).

This distance, called the *gap*, is precise. Incorrect gaps cause misfiring plugs and consequent loss of economy and power. Therefore, care should be taken to keep the plug clean and properly gapped.

Fig. 3-13. A gapping tool is indispensable for correct adjustment of spark plugs and contact points.

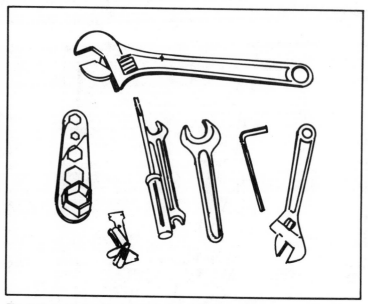

Fig. 3-14. A variety of tools, some especially designed for mopeds, can make repair and maintenance jobs easier.

A spark plug tool is a necessity. Select the correct size part of the tool and slide it into the spark gap. It should scrape slightly across both sides. If the gap is too wide, press the L-shaped prong against a hard smooth surface, such as concrete, and remeasure. If the gap tool won't slide into the gap, pry the points apart slightly with the tool or with a flat-bladed screwdrive. The arm will bend fairly easily; don't use too much force (Fig. 3-13).

Ideally, spark plugs will be clean all the time, but over a period of time, plugs corrode and need cleaning. Scrape the excess deposits with a knife and blow the plug clean with your breath or compressed air. Most repairmen advise against using a sand-based cleaning tool to scrub plugs (Fig. 3-14). They will do a good job of cleaning, but they tend to leave particles of sand deep in the crevices of the plug. Such particles could work loose and damage your cylinder and piston.

Spark plugs are inexpensive. It is more productive and cost-effective to clean a plug with a knife and then replace it after a few such cleanings than it is to worry about dust or sand slipping into the cylinder and scarring it. For more detailed information on spark plug care and how to "read" engine conditions by spark plug wear, see Chapter 7.

Chapter 4

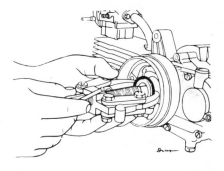

Repairing a Flat Tire

Next to running out of gas miles from a service station, the most frustrating thing that can happen to a mopedder is to have a sudden flat tire. A slow leak generally will be detected soon enough to repair it in a convenient spot, but running over a nail, broken glass, or even a long thorn means a sudden loss of air—even a violent blowout. The moped wobbles, and a quick stop is necessary to prevent losing control and even more damage to the tube or tire.

If that unexpected stop is along a lonely stretch of road, the mopedder is often the only one to repair the flat. It is important for a mopedder to carry a tire patch kit (Fig. 4-1) just as it is vital for a bicycle rider to have one. With the correct tools, a tube can be patched beside the road within a few minutes. Even the bare necessities of a couple of screwdrivers and an adjustable wrench are enough to do an emergency repair.

The most effective repair is one that is never needed. Proper attention to the tires and their needs could mean never having to patch or replace a flat tube. When riding, pay attention to the roadway. Stay away from broken glass. Avoid stray nails. As much as possible, don't ride in or around fields where thorny weeds exist. Even a small goat's head sticker can be pushed through the tire and scratch the tube, causing a slow leak.

Inevitably, a thorn will get into the tread or a small piece of unnoticed glass might be ridden over or—despite the best caution—a nail can puncture the tire and tube (Fig. 4-2). For that reason, a

Fig. 4-1. A tire patch kit allows a rapid job anywhere.

moped rider should learn how to repair or replace his own tubes and tires.

There's another reason for the rider replacing his own tubes and tires: cost. Even the most sympathetic moped dealer must charge a fair price for his time to repair a flat, and that often is more than the cost of the tube itself.

REMOVING THE TIRE

It is easier to remove the front tire of a moped than the back

Fig. 4-2. A nail or tack can penetrate the innertube and cause a blowout.

Fig. 4-3. Remove the speedometer casing before removing tire.

tire because fewer things are connected to the front. As shown in Fig. 4-3, simply remove the end of the speedometer cable (depending on the model, either by pulling it from its socket or by unscrewing the holding nut). Then remove the brake cable by releasing tension on the brake arm (Fig. 4-4). Sometimes a nut must be

Fig. 4-4. The brake arm must be compressed to easily remove the rear brake cable.

loosened, other times, simply unhooking the end of the cable from the brake arm is enough.

Then loosen the axle nuts, remove them, remove the fender supports if they are on your model, and slide the wheel down and out of the fork. It's a good idea to replace the axle nuts at this point so you won't damage the axle threads.

The rear wheel—connected as it is to the drive chain, brakes, and bicycle chain—requires a little more effort to remove. If you are going to repair a flat tube, often it isn't even necessary to remove the wheel completely.

If you are working at home, place the moped on a workbench (Fig. 4-5) or other surface of convenient working height (24 to 28 inches is convenient for most people). Set the moped on its center stand and tie down the front wheel (Fig. 4-6) so that the rear wheel is hanging off the end of the workbench (Fig. 4-7). Balancing the moped on the workbench is important—anchor the front wheel securely, and be aware that if you should completely remove the rear wheel, the balance of the moped will change toward the front wheel.

(Note: If the exhaust muffler is hot, let it cool first.)

The rear brake cable attaches to a brake arm similar to the front brake, or it is pinned between a plate and a nut. Release the brake cable as necessary.

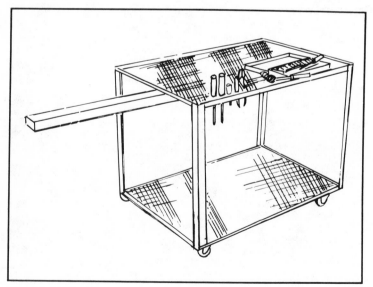

Fig. 4-5. A cart with proper tools at hand makes changing a tire much easier.

Fig. 4-6. Run the moped up a braced incline to the cart.

Fig. 4-7. Use an extension to help support the moped and balance it.

Fig. 4-8. The shock absorbers should be removed from the rear swing arm.

Loosen the axle nuts (Fig. 4-8), but don't remove them. Slip the axle forward on the spring arm to release tension on the chain, and then slip them off the rear sprockets.

On some models, such as the Puch, the brake arm must be slid from its retaining nut. It then can be left hanging out of the way.

Fig. 4-9. After releasing the chain and axle nuts, lower the rear wheel from the frame.

44

Remove the wheel by continuing to slide it forward on the swing arms until it drops free (Fig. 4-9). On some models it might be necessary to remove the axle nuts completely to do this.

Many mechanics advise removing the master clip on the drive chain to remove the rear wheel. That can be done, but it adds an extra step to replacement and is not really an advantage. The chain will hang there without bothering anything.

Reinstalling the wheel is essentially a matter of reversing the steps of removal. Be careful to set the chains squarely on the rear sprockets, and reset the brake arm in its fitting (Fig. 4-10) before completely setting the rear axle back in the swing arm. Carefully adjust the drive chain tension to its proper setting, then reconnect the brake cable, tighten the axle nuts, and recheck the chain tension. If it is not correct, it becomes a simple matter of adjusting it without concern over the remainder of the rear wheel assembly.

WHEEL REMOVAL

It might be necessary to remove a wheel completely from the chassis in order to replace a rim or work on the transmission hub,

Fig. 4-10. The rear brake arm must be slipped over a pin on the rear swing arm when re-mounting.

but merely removing a tube for repairs can be accomplished with the tire and wheel still on the bike. I will show you that and then go on to a more orthodox way of repairing a tube.

If you know that there is a hole in the rear tube and you can locate it easily (a large puncture stands out on even a deflated tube), you can patch the tube without removing the entire assembly. Disconnect the brake cable and chains as above (Fig. 4-11), slide the axle forward on the swing arm. Then remove the tire as shown below. Slip the tube from between the rim and tire, locate the puncture and repair it. Slip the tube back onto the rim and inside the tire and replace the rear assembly as above.

With a little practice, this can become a simple, rapid, and even favorite way of repairing a flat, but too often a puncture is too small to be readily seen and repaired. The wheel has to come off. (The following remarks will apply to either the front or rear tire.)

Use tire tools, such as motorcyclists use, or a set of lightweight bicycle tire tools (these include a notch for hooking them around a spoke—an advantage when a three-handed job has only two hands available). In an emergency, a couple of flat-bladed screwdrivers can be used, but extreme care must be taken that the blades don't scrape or puncture the tube.

Let as much air pressure as possible out of the tube by depress-

Fig. 4-11. Loosen the bicycle chain by releasing pressure on derailleur and slipping the chain away from the sprocket.

Fig. 4-12. Let the extra air out of the tire, if necessary.

ing the air valve (Fig. 4-12). Some recommend removing the valve stem entirely, but that adds another unnecessary step.

Insert a tire tool (Fig. 4-13) between the metal rim and the edge of the tire (called the *bead*). It doesn't matter which side of the tire you work on first, but we'll call the side you start on the front side. Press down on the tire tool (I use screwdrivers in the photographs to show locations and actions better) to force the bead above the edge of the rim. Insert a second tire tool a few inches away from

Fig. 4-13. Start removing the tire from the rim by bringing the bead over the rim.

the first and repeat the process while keeping pressure on the first tool.

Here's the tricky part. If you have only two tire tools (the bicycle tools with the spoke hook generally come three to the set), keep hold of the second tool. Wiggle the first tool loose, trying not to let the bead slip back inside the rim. Move the first tool ahead of the second tool and repeat the process. If you use the three bicycle tools, the process is easier, and the tools remain hooked to the spokes until you move them (Fig. 4-14).

Move around the rim until the entire front side is above the rim (Fig. 4-15). Now remove the valve stem of the tube from its place in the rim. Often a knurled nut must be removed in order for the stem to slide free.

At this point, you can remove the tube simply by pulling it through the front side. The tire remains basically in place on the rim and you can replace the tube easily. If you need to take the tire completely off the rim, do the following.

From the front side, slide a tire tool completely between the rim and tire. Press down (toward the hub). The bead on the back side will come forward and start to move over the front rim. Repeat the process with the second tire tool, and the tire will easily start to come off the rim. Set the rim and tire aside for future inspection (Fig. 4-16).

LOCATING HOLES

Most tubes are black. Holes are dark. On these two facts rest the best way to locate small holes (large holes stand out).

Fig. 4-14. Use at least two tools to help pull the tire off the rim.

Fig. 4-15. Don't let the tools slip, or you may have to start over.

Inflate the tube slightly, just enough to make it round. Hold it in clear water; a good-size pan or a sink will work well. Watch for air bubbles (Fig. 4-17). When you see them, find out where the air comes from and mark the hole (dry the spot and use chalk or light-colored grease pencil). Even if you *know* there is only one hole, and you locate it on the first try, continue searching for others with the same pro-

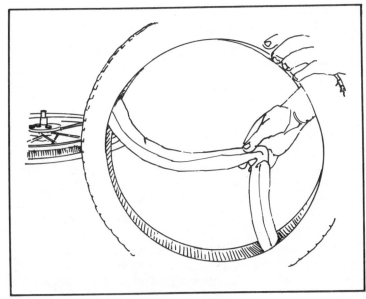

Fig. 4-16. Gently pull the innertube out of the tire.

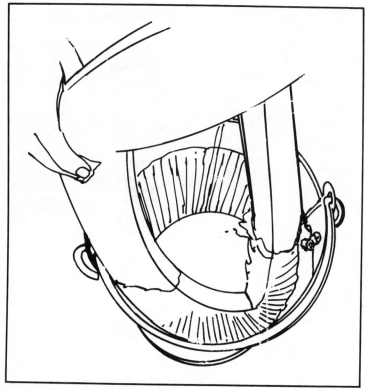

Fig. 4-17. Dipping a partly inflated tube in water can locate tiny leaks.

cess. Nothing has caused more repeats of flat tires than a leak for which the repairman didn't look.

When you have made a complete circuit of the tube through the water and have marked any holes, patch each hole.

PATCHING THE LEAK

A simple patch kit is called a *cold patch repair kit*. It differs from the *hot patch repair kit* in that fire is not used. The hot patch actually melts the rubber patch into the rubber of the tube. The cold patch is not quite as strong, but for most repair jobs the difference really isn't that important. Besides, a cold patch kit is smaller, less expensive, and more easily applied.

The hot patch is applied by first roughing the surface of the tube with a knife edge or a special scraper provided in most repair kits (Fig. 4-18). Don't touch the roughed-up surface; it will weaken the patch.

Peel the protective paper off the patch and place it over the hole, making sure it is centered over the hole. Clamp the tube with the clamp provided. Make sure the fuel container is over the hole and the patch.

Peel up a corner of the fuel container and light it. This is a dangerous process. Don't do it near your moped gas tank or any other flammable area (such as a weed field). At the same time, remember that the patched area and the clamp will be hot. If possible, hang the tube over a tree limb, a braced board, or a nail. Let the fuel completely burn away and let the area cool. When the clamp and tube are cooled, remove the clamp and peel the fuel container off the patched tube.

If you have several small leaks, you might not want to go to the trouble and expense of a hot patch for each leak. If you are in a hurry, try the cold patch method.

Again, roughen the area around the hole. Make the roughed area slightly larger than the patch you will apply. Don't get carried away and dig the Grand Canyon—just rough up the surface.

Many repair kits come with a sized patch and a larger segment of patching material you can cut to size. Kits also contain cement. Spread a small amount over the roughed-up area and a little beyond (Fig. 4-19). Take the patch, precut or cut to order, and center it over the patch, waiting half a minute or so for the cement to dry and become tacky.

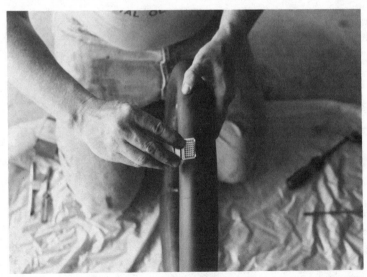

Fig. 4-18. Prepare the tube surface by scraping it lightly.

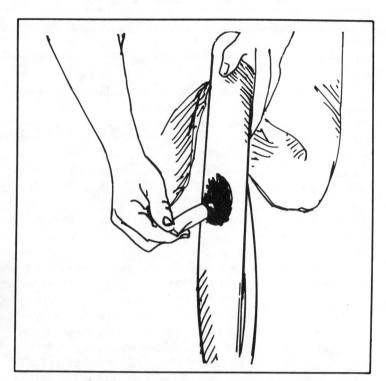

Fig. 4-19. Apply a cement to the area around the hole, being sure the cement will be applied to all the patch.

Fig. 4-20. Set the patch over the cement and hole. Press it firmly.

Take the protective paper off the patch and press it firmly over the puncture and cement until it sets—give it a minute (Fig. 4-20). Smooth the patch with your fingers from the center outward to remove all air bubbles, which can weaken a patch. What you think is a good patch could peel off, even inside a tire, if an air bubble remains.

Sprinkle a little powder on the patch to help smooth the first rubbing on the inside of the tire. Powder hardly ever comes with a repair kit; talcum powder is ideal for the job.

Don't put the tube back into the tire yet. Visually check the rim of the wheel to determine if there is a small piece of metal rubbing on the tube (Fig. 4-21). A spoke might have slipped up inside the rim, or a rim might not have been finished properly. Any small burr should be chipped off and the area rubbed with garnet paper or steel wool.

Now check the tire. If a thorn or small piece of glass caused the puncture, it may still be in the tire, ready to cause another hole. Run your fingers around the entire inner surface of the tire (Fig. 4-22). Be careful! That little piece of glass can cut a finger, too. Then check the tread of your tire. Look carefully between the treads because a thorn could be embedded deep within the tread area.

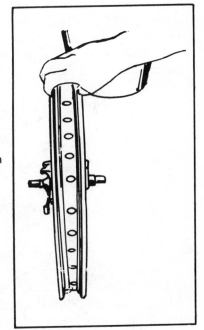

Fig. 4-21. Check the inside of the rim for any burrs.

Remove any foreign matter from inside or outside the tire—even a small, sharp pebble caught in the tread can cause trouble.

Leaks also can occur around the valve stem. In that case, don't waste your time. If the valve stem is leaking, buy a new tube. You can't repair the area around the valve stem, and use your judgment on repairing tubes. If you have repaired a tube three or four (or more) times, chances are it's pretty weak. Get a new one. Check the thorn-proof tubes. These thicker-walled tubes are not puncture-proof, but they will resist a small object, such as a thorn, that scratches the surface of the tube.

TUBE AND TIRE REPLACEMENT

Slightly inflate the tube, just enough so it feels slightly stiff. That makes it easier to handle. Line up the valve stem with the hole in the rim and slip the tube inside the tire. If the tire is still half on the rim, use care that you don't pinch the tube.

Insert the valve stem inside the rim hole. If the stem flops out, add a couple more pounds of air pressure; then replace the knurled nut.

Bring the back side of the tire near the rim. Place the tire tool between the front bead and the rim and lift up, repositioning the tire inside the rim. Repeat with the second tire tool until the entire front bead is inside the rim. As you do so, check to make sure you aren't harming the tube by folding it or slicing it with the tire tool.

Rotate the wheel, with your eyes near the tread. Check that the bead is seated within the rim on both sides, all the way around the wheel.

Fig. 4-22. Make sure the inside of the tire doesn't have foreign objects.

54

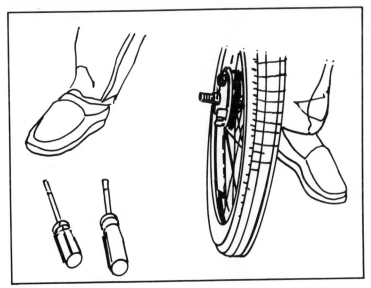

Fig. 4-23. Check the tire pressure before reassembling, even if it is by pressing down on the tire.

Bring the air pressure up to standard, checking occasionally that the bead is seated against the rim, especially when the tire pressure is at maximum.

OTHER TIPS

If you don't have a tire pressure gauge at the moment, use your fingers (Fig. 4-24). Just as with a bicycle, chances are the pressure is correct when the tread doesn't give much when pressed firmly with both thumbs. Another way to check tire pressure is to ride the moped slowly while someone else looks to see if the tire seems to be pressed down on the road surface (Fig. 4-23). If so, add a couple of pounds of air, but don't overpressurize the tire.

You can tell when a rear tire is low when you feel like you are wobbling around your track as you travel. Not much weight is applied to the front tire, but when it is low it is easily noticed. The rider can simply lean a little to one side and look for a lot of rubber on the ground.

Most mopeds use a 2.25-×-16 tire, but a 2.50-×-16 tire will fit. Take care not to let the larger size rub fenders or other parts of the frame. A larger tire will reduce power transferred through the sprocket, but it also will give a slightly more solid-feeling ride.

Chapter 5

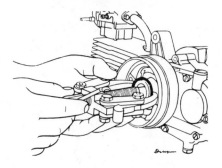

Cables and Their Replacement

While an automobile uses solid metal rods and links to connect operating controls to brakes, steering, and transmission, the moped uses flexible metal cables, not unlike the wire used to hang large pictures. Cables lead from the handlebar assembly to the front and rear brakes, the clutch, the carburetor and the speedometer assembly (Fig. 5-1).

For the use they get, cables are amazingly durable. Because they are hidden in a rubber or plastic sheath, and because they are only links between two more important points, inexperienced moped riders tend to forget about cables until it is too late.

Cables bend, flex, twist, and stretch each time brakes are applied or the throttle is used. The stress is such that they can break within a year if care is not taken to prevent it.

Lubrication and the routing of a cable are the two most important preventive-maintenance devices to assure long cable life—by long, I mean three to four years before the inevitable stretching renders a cable simply too long to use effectively.

Lightweight oil, graphite dust, or special cable lubricant all are used to keep a cable operating smoothly in its sheath. Obviously, the special lubricant is best, and the added cost is worth it over the extended life of the cable. Cable lubricant generally comes in a spray can, with a special attachment available to help lubricate easily.

Routing cables likewise is important. By the nature of pulling on brakes and carburetor, cables require as straight and uncluttered

Fig. 5-1. The maze of cables on the handlebars has a purpose—to give control of the moped to the rider with his hands. Note the lubrication accesses on the two brake cables.

a path as possible. If the cables could be laid out in a straight line, it would be ideal, but the moped would have to be several feet longer and decidedly odd-looking.

So compromises are made. The rear brake cable, as an example, is passed through the handlebar assembly, under the gas tank or main frame, past the pedal assembly, and to the brake arm. This requires two curves, which should be as gentle and sweeping as possible. Any sharp bend results in the cable being forced against the sheath and hanging up. The brake won't work properly.

As close to an ideal cable placement is the front brake cable. It leads from the right-hand grip, through the handlebar assembly, and straight down to the brake arm. If you are careful, you can lean over the handlebar enough to watch the brake arm pull up as you apply the front brake.

The carburetor or throttle cable receives more activity than the brake cables simply because it always is in use. Special care should be taken to see that the carburetor cable is always in top shape. There is nothing more aggravating and final than having a throttle cable break just as you get ready to ride off—and nothing can be substituted for it.

Cable come in different lengths, depending on the moped and

the application. The front brake cable is shorter than the rear brake cable, which has a greater distance to reach.

Cables also will look different. Brake cables have solid metal pieces soldered or welded at each end (Fig. 5-2). These pieces slip into designed grooves in the brake arms and the brake handles. This provides a solid, sure anchor so that the cable won't slip out at an inopportune moment. When the cable unravels or breaks, even near one end, the entire cable is useless. It must be replaced.

A throttle cable has a soldered tip on one end that anchors inside the carburetor and a bare tip in the other end. This end passes into the throttle assembly on the handlebar and can be adjusted for correct tension. As the cable stretches, it is easy to take up the slack merely by loosening the appropriate setscrew and pulling the cable with needle nose pliers.

The clutch cable is a combination of the other types of cables. On the engine end, it has a metal piece like the brake cable, which hooks through the clutch arm and provides security from slipping. The other end is bare and passes through the clutch handle. As in the case of the throttle cable, this end can be easily taken up as the cable stretches; until the cable actually wears out, it can be taken up indefinitely.

LUBRICATION

Let's assume you are using the pressurized cable lubricant and the special lubricating tool that slips onto the cable. Lubrication then becomes easy (Fig. 5-3).

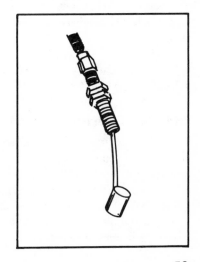

Fig. 5-2. Brake cables have a solid end to hook onto the brake arm. The threaded ferrule allows adjustment as the cable stretches.

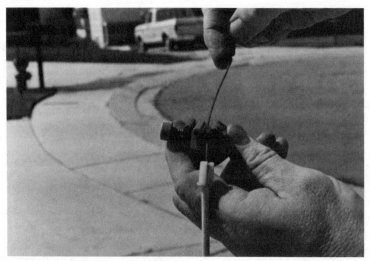

Fig. 5-3. Attach the cable lubricating tool on one end of the bare cable.

Detach one end of a cable, slip the bare cable into the rubber portion of the lubricating tool, and tighten the setscrew. Place the thin plastic tube on the lubricating can into the can's spray hole, then into the lubricating tool. Only a brief squirt is necessary to send fluid through the sheath and dripping out the other end. Be sure the cable, not the sheath, is inside the lubricating tool.

Some sheaths have an access hole built in near one end of the sheath. Flip open the cover and insert the can's plastic tube directly into the access hole (Fig. 5-4). Squirt as before. Remember to close the cover; it keeps out dirt. This access hole can be used for lightweight machine oil in an emergency or graphite can be squeezed in there.

Wipe off the excess lubricant from the extreme end of the cable and reattach. Only a very little lubricant is necessary, but lubricate whenever you feel that the cable is rubbing dry against the sheath.

ROUTING CABLES

It is not difficult to route new cables, when replacement is necessary, if you will mark down the route the cable is to take when you remove the old cable.

You can buy just a new cable if it is a throttle cable or clutch cable. Brake cables usually come in their own sheaths. If you want to retain the old sheath, spray a little lubricant directly on a rag and wipe down the new cable before you insert it. Be sure not to unravel the end as you push it through—do the job gently. If you reuse an old sheath, you probably can leave it in place and insert the new cable easily enough, being mindful of the bends the sheath will take.

If you must remove the entire sheath, make written or mental notes of exactly how the cable is routed. This is especially important in the case of the rear brake cable, which must run the gauntlet of the hot engine and exhaust, the pedal crank assembly, and still avoid getting caught in the chain or the rear wheel. Further, as on the Pinto model of the Puch, the outside engine cover cannot be replaced if the brake cable is lying on the screw mounts, where it tends to fall. A dextrous finger or screwdriver will lift the cable away from the mount, but remember exactly where the cable goes anyway.

To remove the rear brake cable, loosen the ferrule nuts on the handle end and slide the end of the cable from its resting place. Let it dangle. At the brake arm end, squeeze the arm up until the end drops out of its slot (help it along). You may need to loosen two nuts on the cable to get enough play in the brake arm to let the end drop free.

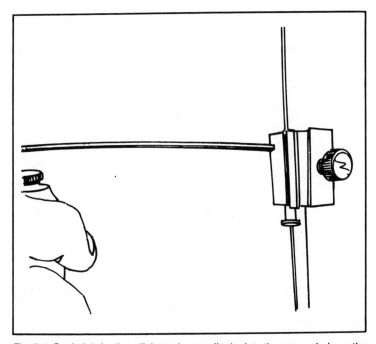

Fig. 5-4. Squirt lubricating oil through a small tube into the access hole on the lubricating tool.

Fig. 5-5. Dropping the front wheel requires taking off the speedometer cable (right side of wheel).

To install a new rear brake cable, start with the brake arm end. Run the cable through its route, and be careful to avoid more bends than are necessary. Squeeze the brake arm so that the cable slips into place. It may be necessary, on some mopeds, to remove a spring in order to set the metal piece of the cable properly. Readjust the set nuts of the ferrule temporarily. At the handlebar end, slip the cable into place and adjust the ferrule to create correct tension.

It is necessary, on both brake cables, to adjust both ends properly. The ferrule on the handlebar end should be as close to the end of the cable as possible to allow for later tension adjustment. Set the two nuts at the brake arm end to allow for maximum future adjustments as necessary. These nuts are called on when the handlebar ferrule cannot be adjusted further.

Removal of the front brake cable follows a similar procedure, but the routing is easier (Fig. 5-5). The cable merely drops through the handlebar assembly and straight to the wheel hub, usually on the left-hand side of the wheel (make sure the cable drops through the handlebar assembly on the correct side of the wheel to avoid one of those unnecessary bends). Frequently, the front brake cable does not have the ferrule and set nuts at the wheel end. The only tension adjustment is by the handlebar ferrule.

The clutch cable is as easy to replace as the front brake cable, but you must gain access to the clutch by removing the cover over the clutch by taking off the outside engine cover and removing the clutch cover. On some models, the arm where the cable attaches is accessible after you remove the engine cover. Merely slip the metal end into the clutch arm and route the cable up through the handlebar assembly. The trick with this job is keeping the lower end in place. Even if the end slips out while you are handling the cable, it can be easily reattached before you replace the upper end on the clutch handle.

When you slip the upper end of the cable through the hole in the clutch handle, be very careful not to buckle the cable, causing the wire to unravel or break. As with any cable, the clutch cable needs to be smooth pulling.

Maneuver the cable all the way through the hole and well past the set screw located in the clutch handle. Make sure now that the clutch arm end is firmly in place, and tug on the upper end until the clutch arm is just ready to move. Keep the cable in that position until you can tighten the set screw.

Properly done, there will be enough cable left over to tuck into a groove provided in the handle (Fig. 5-6). As the cable stretches and is tightened repeatedly, too much cable extends over the handle. It will be necessary to cut off the excess. Use a good wirecutting tool to leave a clean edge, and tuck the remaining end back into place.

Fig. 5-6. The clutch cable slips into a small groove in the clutch handle. You may want to wrap the handle with black tape to keep frayed ends from poking your hand.

Fig. 5-7. Speedometer cables are attached on the underside of this unit.

If you don't have a good wire cutter, do the best you can, but notice that the end will be frayed. To avoid nicking your fingers on the sharp wire, wrap the handle with tape, securing the cable end safely. Most clutch handles are black; a good taping job with plastic electrician's tape will hardly be noticed.

The speedometer cable probably will never have to be replaced, if it is given regular lubrication, because it does not flex very much. Occasionally, though, you must remove the lower end (Fig. 5-7) to work on the front tire. Just remember how it was unthreaded and rethread it the same way. You can lubricate the speedometer cable as you do other cables.

Chapter 6

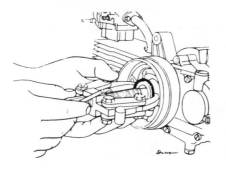

Fuel System

The fuel system is—after the electrical system—the most complex and least understood system on a moped. In addition, there is an element of personal danger involved that is usually underestimated by anyone who has not been in the vicinity of a fuel tank explosion. Some repair operations involve dribbling gasoline from open fuel lines and carburetor float bowls. Do not spill fuel on a hot engine or on a running engine. Work in the open, well away from water heaters, cigarettes, and other sources of ignition. Do not crank an engine that is wetted with fuel; sparking at the contact points can easily start a fire.

The fuel system has these components:

- Filler cap
- Tank
- Fuel valve
- Fuel line(s)
- Carburetor
- Air filter
- Reed valve (Batavus and Peugeot)
- Fuel pump (Velosolex)

FILLER CAP

The filler cap should be fueltight, whether the tank is full or almost dry. Leaks mean that the cap gasket or entire cap must be replaced. Particularly in dusty environments, it is possible for the vent to clog. The engine will run for a few minutes and quit when the fuel level drops, and tank pressure becomes less than atmospheric pressure.

FUEL TANK

The tank may be integral with the frame or detachable. Columbia's and Motobecane's integral tanks bear frame loads: one part has the function of two. On the other hand, should the tank be damaged, one has the option of making a difficult repair or purchasing a new frame.

Contamination

The major problem with the fuel system is contamination. Fuel may contaminate spontaneously with age. Some of the hydrocarbons in gasoline oxidize and settle as varnish and gum. Besides being difficult to ignite, stale gasoline attacks metal and plastics.

Some water is present in all gasoline because of condensation. As water content increases, the fuel turns gray and globules of greasy water settle at the bottom of the tank. Water rusts the steel tank and corrodes the aluminum parts in the carburetor. Rust and aluminum oxide particles eventually detach and score the piston, leaving tiny vertical scratches. Large amounts of water may make the engine hard or impossible to start and can freeze off the fuel line in cold weather.

Dirt and sand can enter by way of a faulty air filter, air leaks between the filter and cylinder, and through careless fuel handling. The piston rings may take on a satiny finish, as if they were lapped (as indeed they were). The piston will show thousands of fine vertical scratches and, in severe cases, the chromium bore will be affected.

Rust is the number one contaminant. If you suspect rust in the fuel—the condition of the piston or an examination of the residue in the carburetor will provide confirmation—drain the tank and inspect its interior with a small flashlight. Turn the light on before you put it over the filler neck and off after you take it away, because the spark at the switch contacts may be enough to ignite the vapors. A safer way is to secure a piece of white rag to a wood dowel or brass rod and swab the floor of the tank. If rust is present, the rag will show it.

There are several things you can do about rust: ignore it and attack the symptom by splicing a miniature filter into the fuel line. (These filters are available from auto parts houses); attempt to clean the tank; or purchase a new tank.

A severely rusted tank should be replaced, because the tank will almost certainly develop leaks. Minor rust can be contained with an inline filter and by keeping the fuel level above the rust line. The filter will catch most rust particles that float free, and the oil in the fuel should prevent further rusting. Tanks that appear sound but are thick with rust can sometimes be salvaged by chemical cleaning. A word of caution: some detachable tanks are crimped together over a layer of plastic sealant. Bendix and other potent cleaners attack the sealant, leaving you with a more serious problem that is almost impossible to correct without replacing the tank. If the tank appears safe, remove the fuel valve, plug the hole, and carefully pour carburetor cleaner into the tank until the rusted area is covered. A half-hour soak should be enough, because carburetor cleaner is potent, dissolving paint and fingers about as readily as rust and carbon.

Leaks

Tank leaks may be caused by impact damage, faulty welds, and severe rust. If rust is the problem, the only practical cure is to replace the tank. Other leaks can usually be sealed with Produit D'Obturation, better known as Peugeot part No. 69158. To use it:

- Mark the leak site with a piece of chalk.
- Disconnect the fuel line and, if possible, remove the tank from the frame.
- Drain the tank completely, tilting it in the direction of the fuel valve.
- Blow out any fuel that remains with compressed air.
- Close the valve and pour 1 quart of trichlorethylene into the tank. Do not use kerosene or any other petroleum-based solvent.
- Shake the tank vigorously for several minutes.
- Drain and collect the solvent for reuse.
- Remove the fuel valve.
- Thoroughly dry the inside of the tank with compressed air.
- Position the tank so that the leak is at the lowest point.
- Pour a 30-cc. bottle of Produit d'Obturation into the tank. This sealant has a shelf life of six months. If the bottle is not full,

the sealant has undergone a chemical change and will not work.

- Allow 48 hours for the sealant to cure. Do not move the tank during this period.

Alternately, the tank can be sent out for welding. This is not a job for a beginner, for even the most vigorous cleaning does not eliminate the risk of explosion. At a minimum, the tank should be flushed with live steam for 30 minutes and flooded with carbon monoxide during the welding operation.

FUEL VALVE

Figure 6-1 illustrates a three-position fuel valve. The longer of

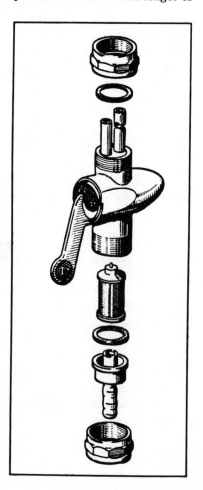

Fig. 6-1. A three-position fuel valve.
Courtesy Butler & Smith.

the two inlet pipes opens in the *on* or *run* position; through the shorter pipe comes the flow when the valve is turned to *reserve*. This particular assembly has its filter screen downstream of the valve; the more common moped practice is to mount the screen over the inlet pipes. Motobecane fuel valves are mounted on the side of the carburetor; other machines have their valves threaded on a nipple on the tank.

The valve should be removed once a year for cleaning. Drain the tank and undo the valve union nut. Some of these nuts are double-threaded: the lower, or valve-side, threads are left-handed; the upper, tank-side, threads are right-handed. They are simultaneously disengaged by turning the union nut counterclockwise. Soak the valve assembly in solvent and work the lever through all three positions. Then blow the mechanism out with compressed air.

FUEL LINE(S)

After several years of service the plastic or neoprene fuel line may grow brittle and develop cracks, particularly at the ends. Quarter-inch fuel line (the size refers to the inside diameter) can sometimes be purchased at auto parts stores. It should not be confused with vacuum or windshield-washer hose, neither or which are fuel-proof. Motorcycle dealers stock clear neoprene hose and clamps. Neoprene slowly deteriorates in sunlight, but is preferred by motorcyclists who want a positive indication that fuel is reaching the carburetor.

CARBURETORS

Moped carburetors are simple instruments, designed for ease of maintenance. There is nothing mysterious about them, but their principles of operation are less than obvious. Some theory is needed, if only to troubleshoot the instrument intelligently.

How They Work

The central principle of all carburetors, moped or automotive, is *pressure diffential*. The weight of the atmosphere presses down on the earth's surface with a force of 14.7 pounds per square inch. During the intake stroke, the engine generates a partial vacuum, where pressure is less than atmospheric, in the cylinder. The carburetor provides the route between engine-induced vacuum and at-

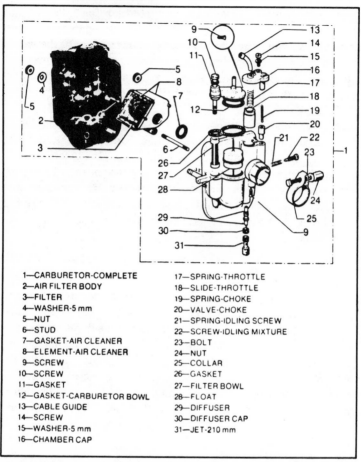

Fig. 6-2. The Motobecane carburetor, developed specifically for moped service.

mospheric pressure, and the pressure imbalance forces air (and thereby, fuel) through the carburetor and into the engine.

A carburetor has three functions. It atomizes the fuel into a fine spray, regulates engine speed on demand from the rider, and adjusts the mixture strength for different operating conditions.

Liquid gasoline burns slowly and inefficiently. To drive the piston, the fuel must be converted into a vapor, so that each hydrocarbon molecule is surrounded by oxygen molecules. Atomization, the process of breaking the fuel into tiny droplets, is the first step toward vaporization. Once atomized droplets enter the engine, they absorb heat and boil off into vapor.

Moped carburetors use a piston slide throttle (Fig. 6-2, part No.

18), connected to the twistgrip by means of a Bowden cable. Withdrawing the piston from the bore allows more air and fuel to pass and, at idle, the piston closes the bore almost completely. The coil spring, part No. 17, forces the piston down, closing the throttle, when the tension on the control cable is relaxed. Without the spring, the throttle could stick open, because cables are flexible and don't "push" well. (In addition to regulating the amount of air and fuel, piston slide throttles have a second and sometimes third function, discussed later.)

The most demanding job the carburetor has is adjusting the strength of the mixture according to the engine's needs. At cruise, an engine is happiest on a mixture of about 16 parts of air to 1 part of gasoline. At high speed the mixture should be slightly richer, in the range of 14 or 15 to 1. The additional fuel is needed to overcome mechanical friction and to cool the piston. At low speeds, the engine again needs a rich mixture to persuade it to run at all, because the cylinder is not very well scavenged, and the incoming charge is diluted by exhaust gases from the last cycle. Idle mixtures may be as rich as 8 or 9 to 1. Cold starting, when the fuel tends to condense back into a liquid, requires very rich mixtures on the order of 4 to 1 or 3 to 1.

The carburetor makes these changes automatically, with no attention from the operator except for starting. This gives some complexity to even the simplest carburetor.

Venturi

Although there is a pressure differential between the carburetor and the cylinder, it is not always sufficient to draw fuel into the engine. A *venturi* or vacuum generator is a restriction in the carburetor bore; it may be streamlined as shown in Fig. 6-3 or it may be quite blunt.

Because just as much air enters the carburetor bore as leaves it, the velocity of the air at the venturi increases over its entry velocity. The boost in air speed helps atomize the fuel, whipping it into a fine mist, but the major benefit is that this velocity increase is "purchased" at the expense of pressure. The pressure of the air stream in the venturi section drops, encouraging fuel to flow into the bore.

Moped carburetors are a little different than those on typical automobiles and small American engines. Instead of forming the venturi as a *fixed* restriction or bulge in the sides of the casting,

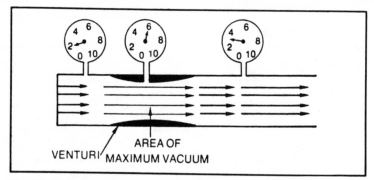

Fig. 6-3. Venturi action. The vacuum gauges read in inches of mercury.

moped designers follow European practice and use a piston to form a *variable* venturi (Fig. 6-4).

At low speeds, the piston masks off most of the carburetor bore, and the area of the venturi—the distance between the lower edge of the bore and the bottom of the piston—is small. Consequently, the air stream moves at high velocity, assuring a good vacuum draw. As the throttle piston retracts, the engine turns faster, and flow velocity is maintained by the increased air intake to the engine.

At full throttle, the venturi effect no longer exists, because the

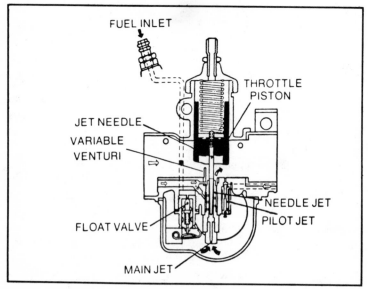

Fig. 6-4. At half throttle, the position and diameter of the needle determines fuel flow through the needle jet.

piston is withdrawn completely from the carburetor bore, but some vacuum is generated by the bore itself. You can demonstrate the principle involved by cutting the ends off a cigar wrapper and blowing through it. The wrapper will collapse because the pressure of the moving air stream in the wrapper is less than atmospheric pressure.

Main Jet

In carburetor terminology, a *jet* is an orifice through which fuel flows. Jets are carefully calibrated so that only a preset amount of fuel flows through them at a given vacuum.

Most of the fuel consumed by the engine passes through the main jet circuit. The circuit is fed from the float bowl and discharges at the vacuum zone created by the venturi. The main jet is inserted at some point in the circuit; it may be just under the carburetor bore or it may be at some distance from the discharge point. In Fig. 6-2 the main jet is shown as No. 31; in Fig. 6-5 it's No. 17. Jets' numbering corresponds to their ability to pass fuel. There is no universal code; each manufacturer has a system of his own. In most cases, the higher the number the larger, more free-flowing the jet.

Bing, Dell'Orto, Jikov, and some other carburetors have a feature borrowed from motorcycles: flow through the high-speed circuit is, in part, controlled by throttle position. A tapered needle on the end of the piston moves up and down in the discharge nozzle, which, in this configuration becomes the needle jet. At low speeds, the piston is low in the bore, and the thickest part of the needle almost fills the jet (Fig. 6-4). Very little fuel flows. As the piston retracts, the needle lifts out of the jet, progressively uncovering it. At full throttle, the needle is almost completely withdrawn and maximum fuel flows. This arrangement provides a richer mixture at high speed and, because the position of the needle is adjustable, gives another opportunity for the carburetor tuner. Needle jet hardware is shown in Figs. 6-6 and 6-7.

Low-Speed Circuit

The *low-speed circuit* discharges just aft of the throttle piston. This auxiliary circuit is necessary because air flow becomes erratic over the main jet as the piston is lowered. Friction losses increase and, at some point while the engine is still running, air through the venturi reaches supersonic velocities. The main jet is caught in series of pressure waves and fuel delivery is unreliable.

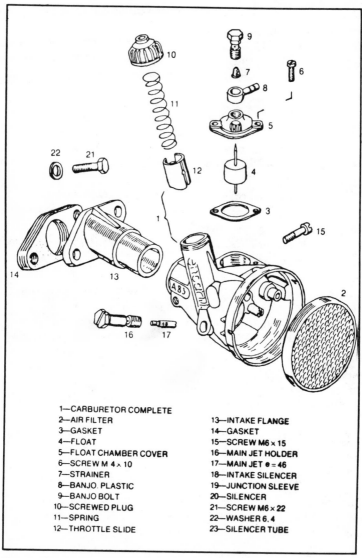

Fig. 6-5. The Encarvi carburetor and silencer as fitted to Tomas bikes.

1—CARBURETOR COMPLETE	
2—AIR FILTER	13—INTAKE FLANGE
3—GASKET	14—GASKET
4—FLOAT	15—SCREW M6 × 15
5—FLOAT CHAMBER COVER	16—MAIN JET HOLDER
6—SCREW M 4 × 10	17—MAIN JET ● = 46
7—STRAINER	18—INTAKE SILENCER
8—BANJO. PLASTIC	19—JUNCTION SLEEVE
9—BANJO BOLT	20—SILENCER
10—SCREWED PLUG	21—SCREW M6 × 22
11—SPRING	22—WASHER 6. 4
12—THROTTLE SLIDE	23—SILENCER TUBE

Figure 6-8 shows a low-speed circuit typical of several moped carburetors. Note the way the throttle needle completely fills the needle jet, denying fuel from that source until the throttle is approximately one-third open. At low speeds the engine runs on fuel supplied by the low-speed or pilot jet.

The term *pilot jet* means that an air screw controls the low-speed mixture. For reasons explained presently, some air is admitted to the jets before the fuel is discharged. This means that the low-speed mixture can be regulated by controlling the flow of fuel or the amount of air premixed in the fuel prior to discharge. Tightening the air screw (on the lower right of Fig. 6-8) reduces the amount of air without affecting the amount of fuel flow. Consequently, the mixture is richer. Turning the needle out has the opposite effect.

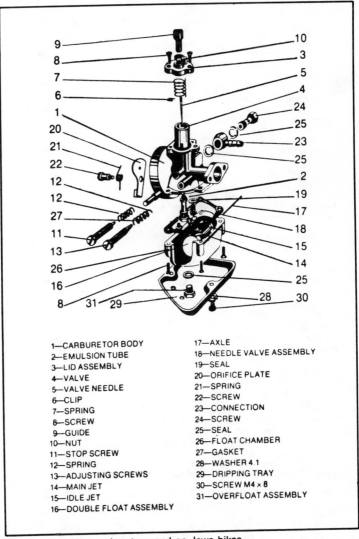

1—CARBURETOR BODY
2—EMULSION TUBE
3—LID ASSEMBLY
4—VALVE
5—VALVE NEEDLE
6—CLIP
7—SPRING
8—SCREW
9—GUIDE
10—NUT
11—STOP SCREW
12—SPRING
13—ADJUSTING SCREWS
14—MAIN JET
15—IDLE JET
16—DOUBLE FLOAT ASSEMBLY

17—AXLE
18—NEEDLE VALVE ASSEMBLY
19—SEAL
20—ORIFICE PLATE
21—SPRING
22—SCREW
23—CONNECTION
24—SCREW
25—SEAL
26—FLOAT CHAMBER
27—GASKET
28—WASHER 4.1
29—DRIPPING TRAY
30—SCREW M4 x 8
31—OVERFLOAT ASSEMBLY

Fig. 6-6. The Jikov carburetor, used on Jawa bikes.

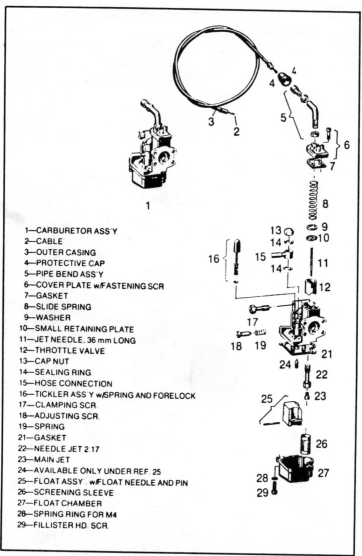

Fig. 6-7. Bing is a famous name in German carburetors, found on such prestige products as the BMW motorcycle. This example is used on the Columbia bike.

Not all moped carburetors employ a pilot air screw; many adjust the low-speed mixture by means of a fuel-regulating screw. The term "pilot" is no longer applicable, and we speak of a *low-speed jet* and a *fuel-regulating screw*. The two screws look alike, although you will generally find a pilot air screw to be blunter and thicker than a fuel-regulating screw. The adjustment procedure is the reverse; tightening the fuel-regulating screw makes the mixture lean.

Air Bleeds

Fuel in both the high- and low-speed circuits is mixed with air before it enters the carburetor bore. The low-speed *air bleed* may be adjustable or not, as discussed above. The high-speed air bleed is fixed. Air enters the high-speed circuit from a port at the carburetor mouth, flows through a passage under the bore, and mixes with the fuel at some point between the main jet and the discharge nozzle.

Figure 6-8 illustrates the typical arrangement. Mixing takes place in the *emulsion tube,* although the same part goes by several names, including main jet holder and diffuser. The emulsion tube is identified by one or more cross-drilled holes in its side. Air enters

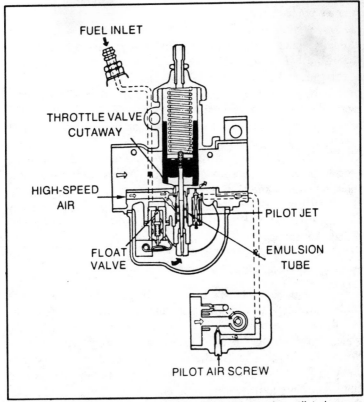

Fig. 6-8. The low-speed circuit is controlled, in this case, by a pilot air screw.

the fuel column through these holes. Should the holes clog, the high-speed mixture goes rich.

There are three reasons for air bleeds: an emulsion of gasoline and air atomizes better than fuel in the liquid state; because each bubble has its own surface tension, emulsified fuel tends to stay put in the passages. Raw fuel would drop away from the jets when the throttle opened suddenly and vacuum momentarily disappeared. The engine would go lean under acceleration.

Again because of surface tension, an emulsion is less likely to siphon into the crankcase.

Float

The Bing float is made of nitrogenated plastic, a foamlike substance that is lighter than gasoline. Gurtner carburetors use a hollow plastic cylinder as the float. The Jikov, a sophisticated design that was developed from the firm's motorcycle carburetors, employs a brass pontoon float.

Once fuel in the bowl reaches a predetermined level, the float closes the inlet valve (Fig. 6-9). This valve is generally known as the *needle and seat assembly*. The needle (Fig. 6-10) is usually made of chrome steel and may be acted on remotely as shown in Fig. 6-9, or may be attached to the float without any intermediary mechanism. The latter arrangement is illustrated in Figs. 6-2 and 6-3. The seat is usually made of brass and, except on the most rudimentary carburetors, is replaceable.

The roof of the float chamber is vented to keep the fuel at atmospheric pressure. Where there is a float adjustment, this adjustment must be made with the greatest accuracy. The distance the float moves before the needle closes determines the level of fuel inside the carburetor. All things equal, the higher the fuel level, the richer the mixture.

Cold Start Provisions

The engine needs a very rich mixture during cold starts. The traditional way to provide this is with a *choke plate* mounted on the mouth of the carburetor bore. The part described as an "orifice plate" (No. 20 in Fig. 6-6) is, in American teminology, a choke plate. When the choke is across the bore, the engine pulls against it, creating a vacuum along the whole length of the intake passage. Both the main and low-speed jets flow.

French designers, in the best automotive and motorcycle tradi-

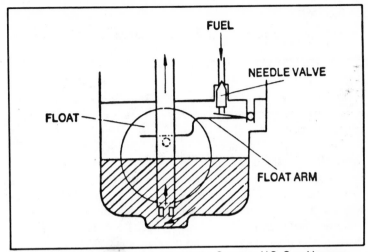

Fig. 6-9. A typical float and remote needle. Courtesy U.S. Suzuki.

tion, use a starting jet, of which the Motobecane carburetor is typical (Fig. 6-2). Two fuel passages leave the floor of the float bowl; the upper passage supplies the main and low-speed jets, the lower passage runs under the carburetor and up to the choke valve (No. 20). The valve is normally kept closed by the spring (No. 19). When raised, the valve allows fuel to flow to a discharge orifice in the aft part of the carburetor bore.

In addition to a choke or a starting jet, some carburetors feature a *float tickler*. The Bing, shown in Fig. 6-7, has this feature. Depressing the tickler sinks the float, flooding the jets for an extremely rich mixture. The tickler should be used with discretion and only on the coldest days.

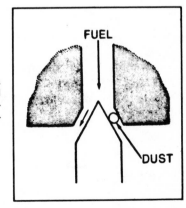

Fig. 6-10. The needle must make a fuel-tight joint with the seat; small particles of dirt or rust caught between these parts will flood the carburetor.

OVERHAUL

Overhaul means cleaning, inspection, and replacement of worn parts. Berkebile 2 + 2 or lacquer thinner will dissolve soft gum and varnish; corrosion and calcified deposits can generally be removed with one of the commercial immersion-type metal cleaners.

Replace the needle and seat, if possible. As mentioned earlier, some moped carburetors have needles that are integral with the float and seats that are part of the float bowl cover. Others have a replaceable soft-tipped needle and pressed-in seat: when the seat wears the parent casting must be purchased.

If the throttle piston is excessively worn, the air will leak between it and the throttle bore. Most carburetors have high- and low-speed adjustments that can be used to compensate for this worn condition; however, extreme wear, signalled by 1/64 inch or so of clearance between the piston and bore, means that the carburetor should be replaced. The needle jet—the brass part that the throttle needle moves in—should not be in contact with the needle and, therefore, should not wear. Unfortunately, this is not always the case. A small misalignment is enough to send the needle into the side of the jet. If this has happened, you will see wear marks on the needle. Both the needle and jet should be replaced. The low-speed adjustment screw should be replaced when it loses its profile (Fig. 6-11). Otherwise, engine idle suffers.

Replace all soft gaskets and O-rings as a matter of course. Hard

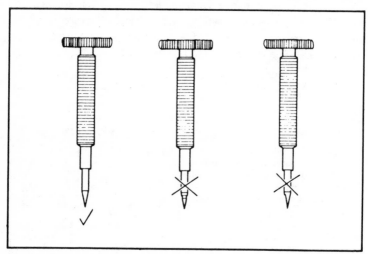

Fig. 6-11. Low-speed adjustment needles can wear out and produce an erratic idle.

gaskets are washerlike affairs found on fuel-line fittings. They may be reused, if they are not grooved. All nonmetallic gaskets should be removed before the carburetor is immersed in a chemical cleaner. Less potent cleaners, such as 2 + 2 Gum Cutter, do not have any immediate adverse effect on gaskets.

Removal

To dismantle the carburetor, first remove it from the engine. It is secured at three or four places:

- Air filter—on many bikes the filter is attached to the frame and connected to the carburetor by a flexible hose.
- Intake pipe—in some instances the pipe must be loosened at the engine end.
- Choke control—if a remote choke is fitted, remove the cable at the carburetor end.
- Throttle cable—disengage at the throttle piston.

The throttle cable mounts at the underside of the throttle piston. Remove the piston cover plate, the part that seals off the top of the piston bore (shown as No. 6 in Fig. 6-7). Most cover plates are secured by small screws; some of the older models used a knurled ring threaded over the top of the carburetor bore. Once the plate is free, carefully guide the piston up and out. Be particularly careful if the piston is fitted with a needle.

Turn the piston over and compress it against the return spring, so the cable end protrudes through the bottom of the piston. Move the free end of the cable through its disengagement slot and allow the piston to pull free of the cable. Bing carburetor needles are held in place by pressure from the return spring acting against a washer and retaining plate. These parts are shown as Nos. 9 and 10 in Fig. 6-7. Once the cable is released, the spring, needle, washer, and retaining plate are free (and easy to lose). Other needle-type carburetors secure the needle with a spring clip: the needle remains in place until the clip is removed. Regardless of the attachment method, note the position of the needle for assembly reference. Typically there are four grooves around the upper end of the needle, and the factory pins the needle at the third groove from the top.

Wipe off the piston with a paper towel or lintless rag soaked in solvent. Vertical scratches on the piston flanks mean that dirt is entering the system from a faulty air filter or a leaking cover gasket. Some discoloration on the bottom of the piston is more or less

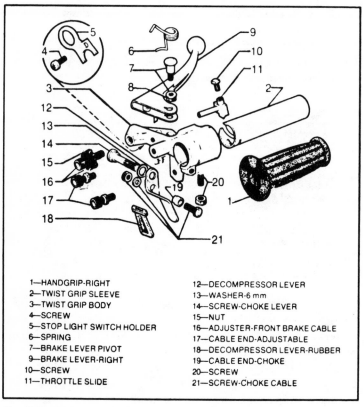

1—HANDGRIP-RIGHT	12—DECOMPRESSOR LEVER
2—TWIST GRIP SLEEVE	13—WASHER-6 mm
3—TWIST GRIP BODY	14—SCREW-CHOKE LEVER
4—SCREW	15—NUT
5—STOP LIGHT SWITCH HOLDER	16—ADJUSTER-FRONT BRAKE CABLE
6—SPRING	17—CABLE END-ADJUSTABLE
7—BRAKE LEVER PIVOT	18—DECOMPRESSOR LEVER-RUBBER
9—BRAKE LEVER-RIGHT	19—CABLE END-CHOKE
10—SCREW	20—SCREW
11—THROTTLE SLIDE	21—SCREW-CHOKE CABLE

Fig. 6-12. Motobecane twist grip and control cable.

normal; heavy carbon deposits may indicate an out-of-adjustment carburetor, perhaps aggravated by long periods at idle.

Inspect as much of the control cable as you can see for frayed, broken, or splayed wires. Replacing the inner core of the cable is usually sufficient for repair; long-term wear, however, can damage the outer sheath. If the throttle binds after a new core has been lubricated and installed, replace both parts of the cable. In any event, the twist grip will have to be partly disassembled. Figure 6-12 shows a typical example.

Lubricate the twist grip threads and the inner cable core. Dab petroleum jelly on your index finger and thumb and draw the cable core between them. A thin coat of petroleum jelly on the grip threads and on the sleeve bearing is sufficient.

At this point, you are ready to disassemble the carburetor. Clean the outside surfaces as a general sanitation measure—dirt on the outside of the casting will invariably find its way to the critical internal parts.

Disassembly

Remove the float bowl or float-bowl cover. The Motobecane carburetor in Fig. 6-2 and the Encarvi in Fig. 6-4 have float-bowl covers; other designs illustrated in this chapter have demountable float bowls.

Remove and discard the float bowl gasket. Disengage the float. A typical pivot pin is shown as No. 17 in Fig. 6-6. Once it is withdrawn, the float and inlet needle can be lifted free. Other carburetors, such as those used by Peugeot, Motobecane, and Tomas have unsecured floats.

Take a close look at the inlet seat. If the seat is slotted for a screwdriver, remove it and the gasket on the underside. Bing and few other carburetors do not have replaceable seats. (The seats are not replaceable unless you purchase the entire float bowl cover.)

Unscrew the main jet, using a screwdriver ground to mate precisely with the slots in the jet. Motobecane and Tomas carburetors have the main jet outside the float bowl for accessibility. The jet is turned with a box-end wrench.

Withdraw the emulsion tube, located in the passage above the main jet. On some carburetors, the tube is held in place by the main jet. A sharp rap on the casting is enough to dislodge it once the jet is removed. Other designs have the emulsion tube threaded into the casting; it is withdrawn with a screwdriver or a small wrench.

Count the turns required to seat the low-speed needle; this is the preliminary adjustment. Now back the needle out and inspect its tip for wear and distortion. Replace if necessary.

Some fuel-line fittings are integral with the carburetor body, others are secured by a gasketed banjo nut. If you are dealing with a banjo fitting, note the position of the inlet pipe before disassembly.

Remove the starting jet from Peugeot and Motobecane carburetors.

It is not necessary to dismantle the carburetor further. Some internal passages are sealed after manufacture with soft plugs or lead shot. In the unlikely event that these passages are clogged—and you can get an idea of their condition from the cleanliness of the parts that are visible—obtain replacement plugs before you disturb the originals. Moped dealers may not be much help, and it's likely you will have to fabricate large plugs from brass sheet and smaller ones from BB shot or brass rod. Seal the plugs with 24-hour epoxy.

Immerse the metallic parts in carburetor cleaner for 20 to 30 minutes. A very dirty carburetor will require a longer soak, but do not park the carburetor in the cleaner and forget it. Eventually the cleaner attacks the castings, leaching the soft metals and leaving you with a porous metal sponge. Once the carburetor appears clean, dip the parts in solvent to neutralize the cleaner.

The most critical aspect of assembly is float adjustment of Bing, Jikov, and other carburetors that use a hinged float. The distance the float moves before it shuts the inlet valve determines the internal fuel level in the instrument. This level affects the air/fuel ratio and is therefore very critical. Unless specifications say otherwise, the float should be parallel with the roof of the float casting (Fig. 6-13). Assemble the needle, seat, float, and pivot pin. Invert the assembly and sight between the float and casting. If the float is not parallel with the casting, make the correction by bending the tang,

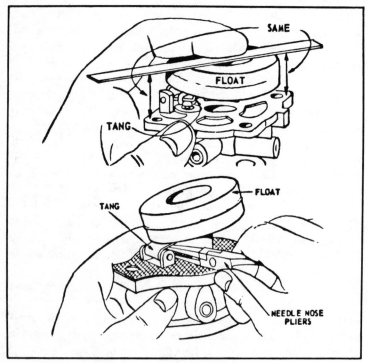

Fig. 6-13. Unless factory literature states otherwise, moped floats are set parallel with the casting.

the torquelike projection between the float and the pin. Use needle-nosed pliers, and do not use the inlet needle as a stop. Pull the float clear of the needle before you apply bending pressure. Steel needles can be damaged by forcing them into their seats; synthetic-tipped needles most certainly will be. Do not twist the float; it must be level and parallel.

Run in the low-speed adjustment screw finger-tight and back it out the number of turns you counted during disassembly. Mount the spring, retaining clips, and other hardware on the back of the throttle piston. Compress the spring and snap the cable into place, passing its end through the piston. Make sure the piston is clean and insert it into the carburetor bore. A slot on the piston flank engages a screw and cast rib on the barrel. Push the piston home, being careful not to force it, because it is possible for the needle to hand on its jet. The piston is assembled dry, without lubricant.

Adjustment

The adjustment procedure is not as complex as it sounds. The first step is to identify the possibilities. All carburetors have some sort of idle rpm adjustment; most have a low-speed mixture adjustment; a few have a high-speed adjustment as well.

Idle RPM. This adjustment controls the height of the throttle piston, regulating the quantity of air and fuel entering the engine with the twist-grip released. If you turn back to the picture of the Bing carburetor in Fig. 6-7, you will see the *pipe bend assembly,* referenced as No. 5. This assembly is capped with a hollow bolt and locknut. The bolt or, more accurately, the barrel nut, is threaded. The control cable casing is moored at both ends, at the twist grip and at the barrel nut. Turning the barrel nut out puts a bend in the cable, making it effectively shorter. The piston rises and idle speed increases. Turning the nut clockwise lengthens the cable and lowers the piston. The locknut secures the adjustment.

A few motorcycle bred carburetors, such as the Jikov shown in Fig. 6-6, have an idle rpm screw that bears against the lower edge of the piston. The barrel nut is still present and is adjusted to give slack so that the distance the piston drops at idle is controlled solely by the screw. One or two designs have no idle-rpm adjustment at the carburetor; the cable is adjusted at the handlebar.

Low-Speed Mixture. When present, this adjustment takes the form of a knurled screw. Most moped carburetors follow European practice and have their low-speed mixture screws across the idle air bleed. This screw, called the *pilot air screw,* controls the amount of air mixed with the fuel. The Bing carburetor is one exception to this: its adjustment screws control the amount of fuel going into the low-speed circuit. The distinction between the two approaches is important: tightening a pilot air screw reduces the air flow and produces a richer mixture; tightening a fuel-control screw reduces the amount of fuel discharged and leans the mixture.

High-Speed Mixture. The position of the tapered needle controls the mixture between one-third and two-thirds throttle. Raising it in the piston puts a thinner section of the needle in the jet, which allows more fuel to pass, enriching the mixture. Lowering the needle fills more of the jet, causing the mixture to go leaner. The factory setting—usually one notch rich—is correct for most bikes. The needle should be dropped a notch at high (over 2000 ft) altitudes and, if only as an experiment, raised a notch for extended full-throttle operation. Raising the compression ratio, removing intake and exhaust restrictions, polishing the head, and other modifications pretty well mandate a one-notch-richer mixture.

The main jet is removable in all carburetors, whether fitted with a needle or not. Under very unusual circumstances it may be necessary to replace the original jet with a different size. This is not a standard tuning procedure and is done only for high altitude operation or when the engine has been modified to give more power. Some moped importers don't stock even standard parts, let alone alternates, and you may have to write the manufacturer to get alternate jets.

On Motobecane and other designs that don't use a needle, the main jet determines mixture strength from approximately one-quarter to wide-open throttle.

Making the Adjustments

The symptoms of carburetor maladjustment are difficult to overlook. An excessively lean mixture bleaches the carbon deposits on the spark plug tip and may cause a flat spot on acceleration. An overly rich mixture soots over the spark plug tip and can induce four-stroking at low rpm. The exhaust beat skips and misses—da da BAM da da BAM. Also, once you've been around engines awhile, you'll be able to smell a rich mixture.

Assume that your carburetor has the full panoply of adjustments and that you have lost track of the original settings. Install a new, correctly gapped spark plug and see that the air filter element is clean. Top up the tank with fresh premix, blended according to the manufacturer's instructions.

Table 6-1. Carburetor Adjustments.

If the carburetor has:	Necessary adjustments are:
No low-speed adjustment screw; no tapered throttle needle on the piston.	Idle rpm.
Knurled low-speed adjustment screw on the outside of the carburetor, just aft of the throttle position.	Idle rpm and low-speed mixture.
Knurled low-speed adjustment screw and tapered needle on the throttle piston. May have main jet options.	Idle rpm, low-speed mixture, and high-speed mixture.

Lightly seat the low-speed mixture screw and back it out one and one-half turns. This should get the engine started. Allow the bike to idle for a few minutes, but not so long that you smell hot metal. Moped engines, even those with forced air circulation over the barrel, overheat when stationary.

Thread in the mixture screw about an eighth of a turn, and wait a few seconds for the mixture change to be felt. If the engine picks up speed, you're moving in the right direction; tighten the screw another small increment. If rpm drops, back the screw out an eighth of a turn past the original setting. Continue to chase rpm until you are satisfied that the engine is running at its peak for that rpm setting. The adjustment is usually broad: tiny changes will not have an obvious effect.

Snap the throttle open about a quarter-turn. The transition from idle should be smooth and effortless. If the engine hesitates, enrich the mixture a smidgen. The idle may be less than perfect, but that is less important than the ability to pull strongly.

Now that the low-speed mixture is correct, it may be necessary to reduce idle rpm. Make this adjustment as described previously. The engine should be turning over smartly, a few hundred rpm under clutch-in speed. An idle so slow you can almost count the revolutions may sound impressive, but it's harmful to the engine.

If the needle adjustment spec has been lost, begin one notch rich. Secure the typical four-groove needle at the second groove from the top. Take the bike out on the road and run it for a few minutes with the throttle between one-third and two-thirds open. Shut off the engine and brake to a stop. The spark plug tip should be brown—the color of coffee with a dash of cream—or tan. Lighter colors mean that the mixture is too lean; the needle should be raised a notch. Darker colors point to a surplus of fuel, and the needle should be lowered. Repeat the test after each change in needle position. With a two-cycle engine, err, if you must, on the dark side. About the worst a rich mixture can do is dirty the spark plug; a lean mixture may destroy the piston.

The main jet controls fuel delivery from approximately one-third to full throttle in carburetors without the tapered needle and from two-thirds to full throttle in those with a metering needle. An oily and carbon-stained spark plug tip after a few minutes at full throttle may mean that the main jet is too large, or that the ignition system is missing at high speed, a condition often associated with the contact points.

By the same token, a lean mixture, one that bleaches the spark plug tip white, can mean that the main jet is too small, that the ignition is advanced beyond specification, or that there is an air leak in the induction tract. An air leak normally shows up at low speeds, but can be compensated for by adjustments. The main jet then becomes a kind of litmus test. If you've unknowingly compensated for an air leak by richening the low-speed mixture, the air leak will be evident when the high-speed jet is in operation.

AIR FILTERS

Most carburetors are fitted with spongelike polyurethane filters. Wire mesh or composition board filter elements are still encountered, but their use is a mark of obsolescence. Polyurethane filters' only required maintenance is cleaning in kerosene or hot water and detergent. Allow the filter to dry and reoil with no more than a teaspoon of engine oil. Knead the oil into the filter until it is completely wetted.

REED VALVES

Batavus and Peugeot engines use reed valves to contain the air/fuel mixture in the crankcase. The Peugeot valve has two reeds; Batavus has four arranged in a triangular housing for maximum efficiency. In the normal order of things, these valves should outlast the engine. When it does occur, failure is dramatic: the engine stops as if someone had turned off a switch. It will refuse to start and the spark plug will remain stubbornly dry after repeated cranking. If you are sensitive to the engine, you may detect a change in the cranking sound.

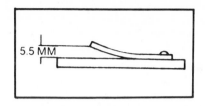

Fig. 6-14. Do not change the backing plate clearance on Peugeot reed valves.

The valve assembly is located on the side of the crankcase, usually under the inlet pipe. It is held by two capscrews and gasketed on both sides. Once these gaskets are disturbed, they should be replaced.

The reeds should be in full contact with the mounting plate or lie a hair's breadth above it. Peugeot reeds have a backing plate, which should not be disturbed for any reason. The correct distance between the backing plate and the mounting plate (Fig. 6-14) is 5.5 mm—more will allow the reeds to open wider and quickly fatigue them. Treat the reeds gingerly, do not touch them at all with your fingers. Look for cracks radiating out from the rivets and for deep pitting along the sealing faces. Using a small screwdriver, open the reeds only wide enough to see what their tips look like. If a reed is missing, it has been injected, and the engine must be torn down to determine the extent of damage.

FUEL PUMP (VELOSOLEX)

A fuel pump might seem out of place on a moped, but the Solex engine rides over the front wheel, where gravity-feed would be impractical. The pump contains a neoprene diaphragm and a plastic check ball. One side of the diaphragm is open to the crankcase and fluctuates with piston movement. Three lines connect to the pump body: the suction line provides fuel from the tank; the return line recycles fuel that is not used by the engine; and the output line connects the pump with the carburetor.

Disassembly

Disconnect the fuel lines and remove the four pump holddown bolts. Lift the pump off (Fig. 6-15). If the plastic seating piece remains on the crankcase, gently pry it free. Replace the diaphragm each time the pump is disturbed. Clean the parts in solvent.

Assembly

Place the plastic seating piece over the crankcase port with the

Fig. 6-15. Removing a Velosolex fuel pump.

concave, or dished, side out. Tap it over the port lug. Without dropping the ball out of its recess, install the pump body. Tighten the screws in a criss-cross pattern to bring the body down square against the crankcase. Connect the fuel lines, running the metal fittings in at least three full turns by hand before you put a wrench on them. Crank the engine a few times; fuel should appear at the discharge port. If everything is satisfactory, connect the pump-to-carburetor hose.

Chapter 7

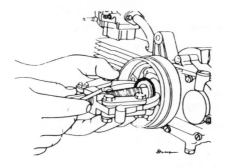

Electrical System

Moped electrical systems are fairly simple, at least in terms of contemporary technology, but the nature of these systems is such that you cannot troubleshoot them or even do much purposeful work on them without some knowledge of the theory. Electrical parts do not make visual sense in the way that mechanical parts do. Almost anyone who looks at a piston comes away with some notion of its function; no one who is ignorant of electricity can understand a capacitor or coil by merely looking.

The theory of these systems is explained in this chapter. Theory may be a bit tedious for someone who has a broken moped, but there are no shortcuts: what is not understood, cannot be repaired.

Here are some ground rules:

● Wiring diagrams are not pictorial. They show what's connected to what as simply as possible, and give you little idea how the actual wires are routed on the chassis.

● Current flows from negative to positive; that is, it moves from the negative terminal of the generator back to the positive terminal. This path is called a *circuit*.

● For current to flow, the circuit must be complete and uninterrupted. A seemingly insignificant break, a few thousandths of an inch between switch contacts, a film of rust, or a smudge of oil can open the circuit.

• The circuit may consist of insulated wire, or it may combine wire and the engine or frame. The junction between the insulated side of the circuit (called the "hot" or "live" side) and the metal parts of the bike is a ground. In wiring diagrams, ground connections are symbolized ⏚ or ⎇ .

• Current will always take the easiest path back to the generator. Each circuit load—coil, horn, lamp, etc.—has resistance to electron flow. If possible, current will find a way to bypass, or short, the load. The problem is particularly severe when part of the circuit is grounded: any uninsulated part of the hot side will short to ground on contact with metal.

IGNITION SYSTEM

The ignition system generates a spark with enough voltage to ignite the air-fuel mixture in the cylinder and times that spark to occur at some preset distance before the piston reaches top dead center.

SPARK PLUG

The spark plug is the final component in the ignition system and is, by far, the most stressed. Combustion temperatures heat the firing tip to $1700\,^\circ$ F during normal operation; engine vibration can generate forces of as much as 50G; and while it is being heated and shaken about, the spark plug must contain combustion pressure and still do its primary job of releasing a spark across a high-pressure atmosphere of oil, gasoline, and air. A faulty plug can make starting more difficult or prevent it entirely. It may cause the engine to miss. A less-than-perfect spark plug can take the edge off performance without causing a noticeable miss: the engine will start easily, accelerate smoothly, yet go flat under full throttle.

It's not surprising that many experienced mechanics change the spark plug before they do anything else to the engine.

Construction

Figure 7-1 illustrates basic spark plug construction and nomenclature. The plug shown is a Japanese NGK, which shares its plated finish with Champion and is otherwise quite similar to most American and German types. Here is a brief rundown of functions.

• Terminal nut—detachable on mopeds and European small engine applications generally.

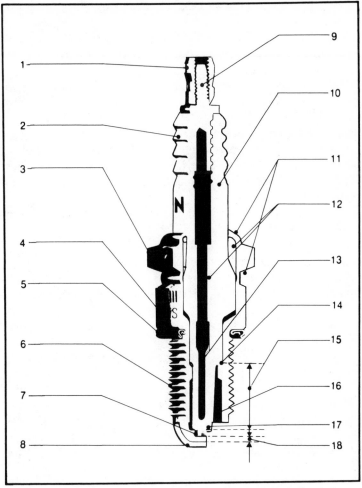

Fig. 7-1. Spark plug nomenclature. Courtesy NGK Spark Plug Co., Ltd.

● Corrugation—protects against high voltage flashover, the same principle used on insulators for high-voltage transmission cables.

● Metal shell—offers purchase for the wrench and support for the spark plug components; 5/8-inch hex is standard.

● Plated finish—for rust protection, generally preferable to a blued finish.

● Gasket—seals the combustion gas.

● Thread—diameter is expressed in millimeters, and the reach (the distance from the gasket flange to the end of the threads), is expressed in fractions of an inch. These dimensions are fixed by the engine maker.

- Center electrode—usually thought of as the "hot" electrode, although in actual fact the direction of the spark is from the ground to the center electrode.
- Ground electrode—sometimes called the side electrode, is grounded to the engine.
- Stud—fixed to the insulator. If the stud is loose, the spark plug must be replaced.
- Insulator—the part old-line mechanics call the porcelain because that was the material originally used. Today, the insulator is made from fused aluminum oxide, a very hard ceramic, akin to rubies and sapphires.
- Caulked portion—part of the defense against leaks between the insulator and shell.
- Sealing powder—a kind of self-sealing gasket which compensates for the unequal rate of expansion of the shell and the insulator.
- Copper core—NGK claims cooling benefits; most manufacturers use a steel core.
- Inner gasket—the first line of defense against internal leakage.
- Insulator nose—the part that has the most effect on the plug's operating temperature.
- Gas volume—the space between the insulator and shell.
- Insulator (firing end)—the nature and color of deposits on the firing end of the insulator reveal engine and combustion-chamber operating conditions.
- Spark gap—the only adjustment normally made on a spark plug.

Heat Range

There are three basic variables in spark plug design: thread diameter, reach, and heat range. Thread diameter is hardly worthy of comment, except to say that it is impractical to salvage a stripped moped head by cutting threads for a larger spark plug.

The reach is calculated to bring the firing tip even with the roof of the combustion chamber. A plug with insufficient reach will have its tip buried in the spark plug port, where it is remote from the action. Starting may be difficult and power will be down because of the additional clearance volume in the cylinder. A spark plug with excessive reach is almost sure to be hit by the piston.

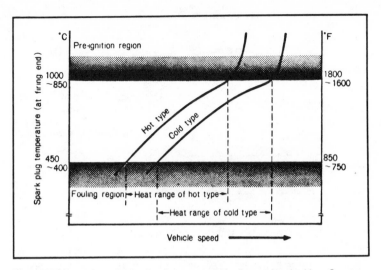

Fig. 7-2. Heat range walks the line between cold fouling and preignition. Courtesy NGK Spark Plug Co., Ltd.

Heat range refers to the cooling capacity of the spark plug. As you can see from Fig. 7-2, the ideal temperature for any spark plug is between 750 and 1800° F. Below this temperature, the firing tip carbons over and fouls; above it, the tip glows and can ignite the mixture early, before the spark occurs.

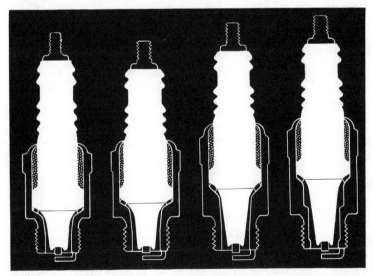

Fig. 7-3. Champion spark plugs in a heat range progression from (L) cold to hot (R).

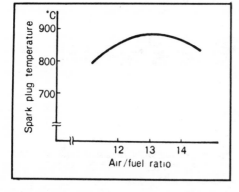

Fig. 7-4. The most power-efficient air/fuel ratio (around 13:1) releases the most heat in the chamber.

Figure 7-3 shows four spark plugs in cutaway view. The plugs have identical thread diameters and reaches, but different heat ranges. The spark plug on the far left is the coldest; the heat range gets progressively hotter to its right. The primary difference is the distance heat travels along the nose of the insulator to the metal shell. Cold plugs have a short thermal path and cool down quickly; hot plugs have a longer thermal path and generally have a greater gas volume between the insulator nose and the inside of the shell.

Spark plugs are available in a wide variety of heat ranges. In general, what determines the choice of heat range for a particular engine is the temperature of the combustion chamber. Hot-running engines need cold plugs, and vice versa.

Heat range selection depends upon:

● The amount of carbon buildup in the cylinder. Carbon deposits can insulate the chamber, trapping heat.
● The air/fuel ration. The ideal air/fuel ration, the ratio that delivers the most power, also generates the most heat (Fig. 7-4).

Fig. 7-5. Each degree of ignition advance entails higher chamber temperatures.

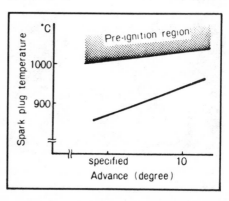

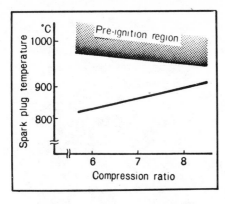

Fig. 7-6. A high compression ratio means power and high temperature.

● Ignition advance. Within limits, additional ignition advance means more power. But each degree of advance takes its toll as heat (Fig. 7-5).

● Compression ratio. The higher the compression ratio, the more efficient the engine, and the hotter the chamber (Fig. 7-6).

● Spark plug tightening torque. Undertorqued spark plugs run hot because heat transfer depends upon the seal between the plug shell and the cylinder head (Fig. 7-7).

The spark plug furnished with the machine is a good choice for average use, but may not be if you've modified the engine for more power. Polishing the cylinder head and piston, smoothing the port profiles, boosting the compression ratio, increasing spark advance, and precision-tuning the carburetor mean higher combustion-chamber temperatures. Depending on the effect of modifications, the original spark plug can become a time bomb, waiting to go into preignition, with the result shown in Fig. 7-8.

Fig. 7-7. A spark plug that is under-tightened overheats. Courtesy NGK Spark Plug Co., Ltd.

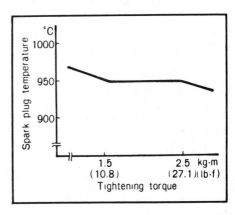

Fig. 7-8. The woeful result of preignition.

Service

Disconnect the spark plug cable by grasping the insulating boot and giving it a half-twist (Fig. 7-9). Moped spark plugs accept a 5/8-inch deep-well socket, sized to clear the insulator (Fig. 7-10).

Spark plugs wear out in 3000 miles or so of moped service. The electrodes round off, erode and eventually become so fine they can overheat and send the engine into preignition (Fig. 7-11). A slightly worn plug can be cleaned, filed, gapped, and used again.

The purpose of cleaning is to remove carbon deposits that can short out the spark, shunting it to ground before the plug fires, or build up in the gas volume area, forming a second spark gap deep inside the plug (Fig. 7-12). In either case, engine performance suffers.

Fig. 7-9. To remove the spark plug cable, give the boot a twist and pull.

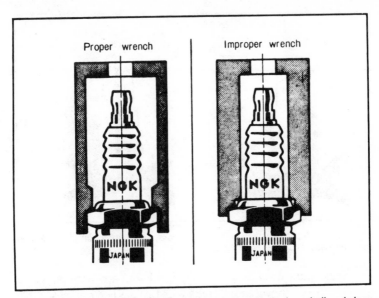

Fig. 7-10. The socket wrench must be in full contact with the hex shell and clear of the fragile insulator. Courtesy NGK Spark Plug Co., Ltd.

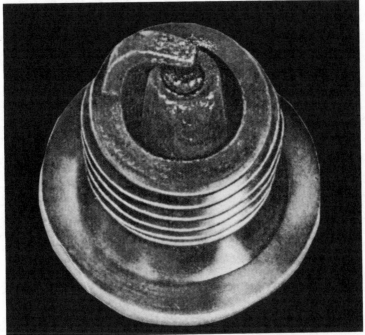

Fig. 7-11. A worn-out spark plug. Courtesy Champion Spark Plug Co.

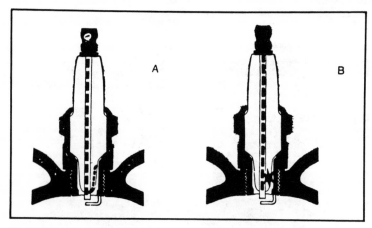

Fig. 7-12. Two maladies that can be corrected by cleaning: fouling (view A) and tracking (view B). Courtesy Champion Spark Plug Co.

Spark plugs may be cleaned by hand with a wire brush and a small knife or screwdriver. Results with this method are reasonably good. The professional approach is to use a sandblaster adapted to spark plug work. The plug is placed in the machine and wobbled under the blast so that the abrasives scrub deposits from the inside of the shell and insulator nose.

In theory, a sandblasted spark plug is as good as new; in practice this may not be the case. Abrasives do not have much effect on lead fouling, a kind of translucent patina that forms on the insulator and causes misfire during acceleration. The newly cleaned plug will behave normally for a few miles and then misfire, costing 500 rpm or so at wide-open throttle. In addition, one must be very careful to remove all of the abrasive before the spark plug is put back into the engine. Even a few particles can do serious damage to the piston, rings, and cylinder bore. It's good practice to blow the plug clean, and then let it soak for a few minutes in lacquer thinner.

After cleaning, reform the center electrode by filing it flat. In Fig. 7-13, the side electrode is straightened so that the sandblast can reach all areas of the insulator nose. This practice is favored by Japaneses mechanics, but is frowned on here; bending weakens the side electrode.

Using a round feeler gauge, gap the plug to specification (Fig. 7-14). The gauge wire should pass between the center and side electrode with a light drag. If it binds, use the bending tool on the gauge to open the side eletrode; if the gauge passes through without

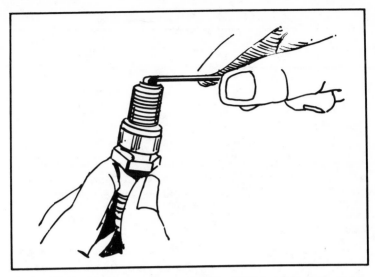

Fig. 7-13. File the center contact flat. Courtesy NGK Spark Plug Co., Ltd.

touching both electrodes, tap the center electrode on something hard. With a little practice, you will be able to correctly gap a spark plug in a few seconds.

Clean the spark plug threads with a hand-held wire brush, not a power-driven wheel that could deform the thread edges. Wipe any carbon or oil deposits from the spark plug port in the cylinder head.

Run the plug in by hand until the gasket bottoms. If you cannot turn it this far with your fingers, turn the plug at least two full revolutions before you apply the wrench. Otherwise, the spark plug may cross-thread and ruin the cylinder head.

Once the gasket is in contact with the head casting, one-half or three-quarters of a turn with a wrench is enough to secure it. Ideally, you should use a torque wrench to tighten the plug to the

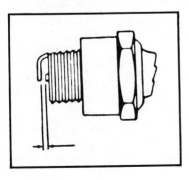

Fig. 7-14. Bend the side, or ground, terminal to adjust the gap. The specification is for Sachs-powered Columbia mopeds.

Table 7-1. Spark Plug Torque Specs.

Spark Plug Thread Diameter	Torque
10 mm	86-104 inch-pounds (1.0-1.2 kilogram-meters)
12 mm	125-175 inch-pounds (1.5-2.0 kilogram-meters)

following specifications. The specs are for a cold engine and should be used only if you don't have the specs for your engine (Table 7-1).

Reading

Reading the spark plugs is the time-honored way of determining combustion chamber temperature and, by extension, of tuning the engine. The basic principle is that the hotter the chamber, the whiter the spark plug tip. If the plug has the correct heat range, the color of the insulator nose should be neutral—either a rich tan or light brown. If temperatures are too high, the nose will turn white and may blister. In extreme cases, the side electrode can show blue temper marks. On the other hand, low chamber temperatures leave a fluffy black carbon residue on the nose.

The difficulty is getting consistent readings. A perfectly well-behaved spark plug will bleach white on a steep, full-throttle hill. The same plug will carbon during an extended period of idle.

Ignition system operation is usually checked by running the bike wide open for a short period, thereby subjecting the plug to max-

Fig. 7-15. Normal: light tan or brown, electrode wear limited to the spark zone.

Fig. 7-16. Gap-bridged: a common malady of two-cycle engines, believed to be caused by dust. Wipe the whisker off and restart.

imum thermal stress, but carburetor tuning is best checked by operating the engine at a number of throttle positions and rpm ranges. In any event, the engine must be brought up to operating temperature and run for a quarter-mile or so at the desired speed. Shutdown must be abrupt in order not to leave false deposits. Chop the throttle, hit the kill button, and brake to a stop. Remove the spark plug and, holding it in the socket wrench to protect yourself from burns, compare the tip with the photographs in Figs. 7-15 through 7-20.

MAGNETO IGNITION

Figure 7-21 illustrates a typical moped *magneto*. The basic parts are:

● Stator plate that secures the stationary magneto parts to the engine block (3).
● Contact points, which trigger the spark (7).
● Exciter coil, which generates primary voltage (12).

Fig. 7-17. Wet fouling: damp black carbon coating over the entire firing end. May form sludge if the condition is chronic. Check spark plug heat range (the plug may be too cold), air/fuel ratio (too rich), fuel/oil ratio (too much oil), ignition system (misfiring). Courtesy Champion Spark Plug Co.

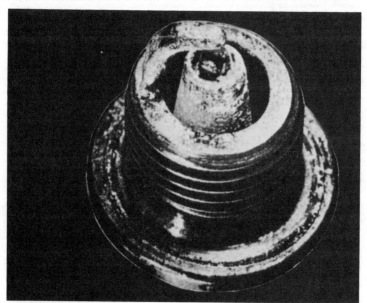

Fig. 7-18. Overheating: electrodes badly eroded, premature gap wear, gray or white insulator. Check spark plug heat range (too hot), ignition timing (too much advance), air/fuel ratio (too lean). Courtesy Champion Spark Plug Co.

Fig. 7-19. Preignition: melted electrodes and in most cases, a white insulator. The insulator may be discolored due to a fog of debris in the overworked cylinder. Check for correct heat range, adequate lubrication, and for overadvanced ignition timing. Correct the problem before the engine is put back into service. Courtesy Champion Spark Plug Co.

Fig. 7-20. Scavenger deposits: brown, yellow, or reddish deposits on the firing tip. These deposits are left by additives in the fuel and are not in themselves dangerous. Clean and return the plug to service. Courtesy Champion Spark Plug Co.

- Cam that rotates against the movable point arm and separates the contacts (16).
- Rotor, which acts as the flywheel and bears permanent magnets (17).
- Spark plug cable (20).
- Ignition coil (21).

Figure 7-22 shows the Robert Bosch magneto, widely used on German and Italian machines. It combines the *exciter* and *ignition coil* in a single assembly. Figure 7-23 shows one version of the CEV magneto, which can be interchanged as a unit with the Bosch.

A diagram of the ignition side of the circuit is shown in Fig. 7-24. The exciter, or primary ignition coil, consists of several hundred turns of enameled copper wire, mounted on an iron form. One end of the exciter coil is connected to the ignition coil, which is mounted on the frame, outside of the magneto proper.

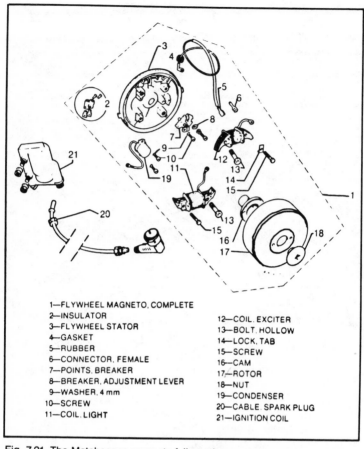

1—FLYWHEEL MAGNETO, COMPLETE
2—INSULATOR
3—FLYWHEEL STATOR
4—GASKET
5—RUBBER
6—CONNECTOR, FEMALE
7—POINTS, BREAKER
8—BREAKER, ADJUSTMENT LEVER
9—WASHER, 4 mm
10—SCREW
11—COIL, LIGHT

12—COIL, EXCITER
13—BOLT, HOLLOW
14—LOCK, TAB
15—SCREW
16—CAM
17—ROTOR
18—NUT
19—CONDENSER
20—CABLE, SPARK PLUG
21—IGNITION COIL

Fig. 7-21. The Motobecane magneto follows the general moped practice with a single lighting coil and two ignition coils. The exciter coil is housed under the flywheel and provides current for the frame-mounted ignition coil.

Operation

The flywheel has permanent magnets bonded to its rim. As the flywheel turns, the magnets sweep part the exciter coil, permeating its windings with magnetic lines of force. When a conductor—and the coil windings are a conductor—is subjected to a moving magnetic field, a voltage is generated in the conductor. The magnetic field must be moving: when the flywheel is stopped, no voltage is produced. At high speed, the exciter coil delivers as much as 300 volts to the ignition coil. Voltage is not constant. It depends upon the proximity of one of the magnets to the coil and upon the position of the contact points.

106

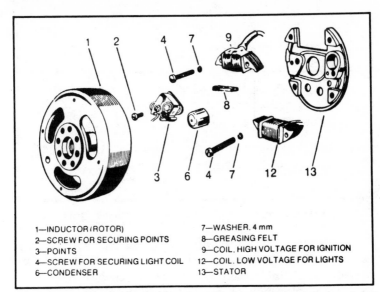

1—INDUCTOR (ROTOR)	7—WASHER. 4 mm
2—SCREW FOR SECURING POINTS	8—GREASING FELT
3—POINTS	9—COIL. HIGH VOLTAGE FOR IGNITION
4—SCREW FOR SECURING LIGHT COIL	12—COIL. LOW VOLTAGE FOR LIGHTS
6—CONDENSER	13—STATOR

Fig. 7-22. The Bosch Model KB6-B212 magneto is unique among mopeds in that the two ignition coils are wound together. Courtesy Cimatti Ltd.

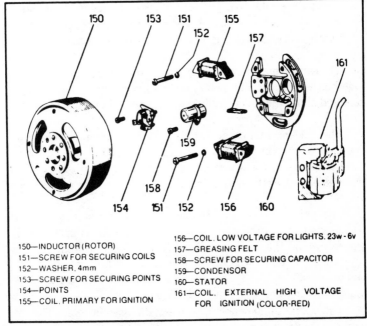

150—INDUCTOR (ROTOR)	156—COIL. LOW VOLTAGE FOR LIGHTS. 23w - 6v
151—SCREW FOR SECURING COILS	157—GREASING FELT
152—WASHER. 4mm	158—SCREW FOR SECURING CAPACITOR
153—SCREW FOR SECURING POINTS	159—CONDENSOR
154—POINTS	160—STATOR
155—COIL. PRIMARY FOR IGNITION	161—COIL. EXTERNAL HIGH VOLTAGE FOR IGNITION (COLOR-RED)

Fig. 7-23. The CEV Model 6932 can be substituted for the Bosch as a complete assembly. Courtesy Cimatti Ltd.

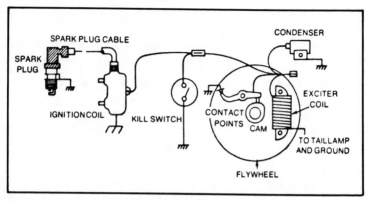

Fig. 7-24. The complete magneto circuit with kill switch and ignition coil.

The points amount to a switch, connected in parallel with the exciter coil. The stationary contact is grounded to the stator plate; the movable contact is insulated and "hot." When the movable contact rests against the stationary contact, exciter coil output passes to ground: no voltage goes to the ignition coil. As the flywheel turns, it opens the movable contact, denying ground to the voltage impressed on the exciter coil. The voltage goes out "seeking" a ground, and it finds it in the ignition coil. The moment of point opening coincides with (and causes) the ignition pulse and is the reference point for timing the engine.

The cam, contact points, exciter coil, and flywheel magnet work together as a team. The points open when a flywheel magnet is centered above the exciter coil, at the moment of greatest magnetic flux.

The condenser (or capacitor) is an electrical buffer. As the points crack open, current will flow, arc across the open points, and burn them in the process. The condenser momentarily absorbs these electrons and releases them back into the circuit when the points close again.

The ignition coil (Fig. 7-25) is also known as the pulse generator. It consists of two windings: fairly heavy enameled copper wire is wound around the form 400 times (the primary winding) and is covered by 20,000 turns or so of extremely thin wire (the secondary winding). The secondary winding terminates at the spark plug cable and delivers 15,000 to 23,000 volts.

The operation depends upon magnetic lines of force. The exciter coil sends, in one magneto, 300 volts into the primary winding. As the winding becomes saturated, it sends out magnetic lines of

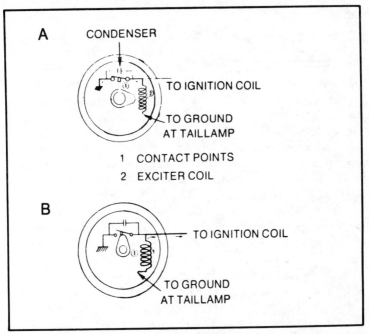

Fig. 7-25. The basic ignition circuit. When the points close, current flows through the exciter coil, its circuit completed through the grounded points at one end and the grounded taillamp at the other (view A). When the points open, current diverts to the ignition coil and the spark plug fires (view B).

force, that move like the ripples on a pond. These moving lines of force cut through the second winding and generate a voltage in it that is proportional to the ratio of turns in the windings.

Spark Testing

Disconnect the spark plug cable at the spark plug by giving the boot a quarter twist and pulling. Do not pull on the wire. Insert a screwdriver into the boot so it makes contact with the cable terminal. Holding the screwdriver by its insulated handle, maneuver it to bring the blade within three-eights of an inch of one of the cylinder fins. Turn the switch on and have a helper turn the pedals. If all is right, the spark will appear between the blade and the fin.

Observe the spark. It should be heavy, thick, and bright blue. A "nervous" spark, one that seems to go in all directions, means ignition problems, particularly if the spark is red or white. A really healthy system will deliver a spark that you can hear like a miniature thunderclap.

Service

The first step is to remove the flywheel nut. The flywheel must be held against wrench rotation. Most flywheels have access ports that accept a pin wrench (Fig. 7-26). In those few cases where the flywheel is closed and shrouded so there is no wrench purchase on its external surfaces, you can hold it with the starting clutch. Because the clutch will slip under wrench torque, shock the nut loose by giving the wrench handle a sharp rap with a hammer. A better method is to fix the piston with a tool that threads into the spark plug port. Break off the insulator on a discarded spark plug and have an extension brazed on its tip. With the tool in place, the piston contacts the extension at the top of its stroke.

Once the nut and lockwasher are loose, the *flywheel* must be withdrawn from the crankshaft stub. There are four ways to do this.

Purchase the appropriate flywheel puller from your dealer, the moped importer, or from a bicycle shop. Some of these pullers are identical to European bicycle crank tools.

Run the nut down flush with the end of the crankshaft and shock the flywheel off with the help of a brass bar and a hammer. Position the bar square against the end of the shaft and hit it hard. This method is more dangerous than using a threaded knocker, because misalignment of the bar can snap the crankshaft stub.

Run the nut down flush and strike the crankshaft end with a hammer. This technique is emphatically not recommended, because it does violence to both the shaft and the nut.

Any technique that shocks the flywheel loose involves the possibility of bending or breaking the crankshaft and scrambling the flywheel magnets. If the flywheel is stubborn, stop work until you can obtain a proper puller.

The most critical area of the flywheel is the fit of the crankshaft

Fig. 7-26. Many flywheels have "windows" that accept a pin wrench. Courtesy Steyr Daimler Puch.

key. The key must be reasonably tight in both flywheel and crankshaft keyways; play between the key and its mating surfaces allows the flywheel to turn relative to the crankshaft and destroys one aspect of magneto timing. If the wear is relatively minor, the flywheel can be centered over the key and tightened down hard; if keyway wallow is severe, the flywheel and the crankshaft must be replaced.

Not all manufacturers supply crankshaft nut torque limits, but 25 ft-lb is an appropriate figure.

The *points* are the most vulnerable part of the magneto and should be considered as sacrificial items, with a life of less than 100 hours. Point failure can make starting difficult, cause misfire at high speed, or disable the engine altogether. Figure 7-27 illustrates a Bosch two-piece point set.

Examine the point set for physical damage: breakage, wear on the rubbing block, excessive clearance between the movable arm bushing and its pivot, and spring misalignment. On some installations, the spring can come into contact with the stator plate, grounding the ignition.

With a screwdriver, pry the movable arm away from the fixed contact. Inspect the contacts very carefully. The tungsten should be dull gray, with the contact faces slightly irregular and puddled. Replace the point set if the contacts look as if they have been torn apart, or if they are any color other than gray. Dark slashes under the points mean that too much grease has been used on the cam or that the crankshaft seal is passing oil into the magneto.

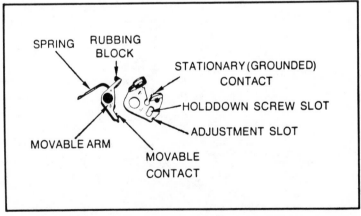

Fig. 7-27. A Bosch two-piece point set. Some sets have the movable arm secured permanently to the pivot post. Courtesy American Parts Co., Inc.

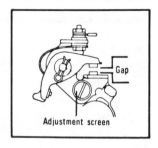

Fig. 7-28. The point gap is the distance contacts open at full extension. The gap on this point set is adjusted by means of an eccentric screw.

To install a new point set, follow these steps:

● Remove the screws that hold the contact assembly to the stator plate and magneto side. Do not lose the lockwashers.

● Lift the point set off the stator and disconnect the wire at the movable arm spring.

● Wipe the point-mounting area of the stator plate with a rag dipped in laquer thinner. Oil between the point set and the stator can deny the ground connection.

● Connect the coil wire to the replacement point set.

● Mount the replacement point set on the stator plate, indexing any pins on the plate with holes in the stationary point assembly.

● Run in the holddown screw(s) a few turns by hand and snug with a screwdriver. Tighten enough to overcome spring tension, but not so much as to make adjustment impossible.

Adjusting the point gap is a critical operation and must be done with precision (Fig. 7-28). The adjustment is by way of an eccentric screw or, more commonly, a screwdriver slot on the stationary contact assembly. The ignition cam may be secured to the crankshaft

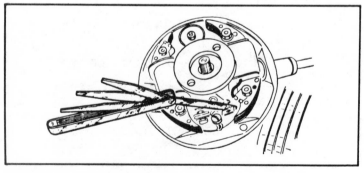

Fig. 7-29. The cam on the Motobecane magneto is located on the hub, allowing easy access to the points.

stub as shown in Fig. 7-29, or it may be integral with the flywheel (on the Bosch pattern). In the latter case, when the cam is part of the flywheel, the adjustment is made after the flywheel is installed (Fig. 7-30). Place the wheel on the crankshaft stub, aligning the key. Working through one of the flywheel windows with a screwdriver, raise the movable contact so that it can ride on the cam. Otherwise, the contact may be jammed as you push the flywheel home. Watch the point contacts as you turn the flywheel: near the end of piston travel, the points will part, reach their full extension, and begin to close. The interval at full extension is the *point gap.*

Point gap specifications are listed in Table 7-2. Select the appropriate feeler gauge blade and wipe it with a shop towel. Do not run the blade between your fingers. The oil on your skin, transferred to the blade and then to the contacts, is enough to disable the ignition. Insert the gauge between the points—the correct gap will produce a slight drag on the feeler. Adjust with the slot or screw provided, holding the feeler gauge in place as you move the stationary point towards or away from the movable point.

Once you are satisfied that the gap is set, tighten the holddown screw. Recheck the gap, because it will have moved a few thousandths of an inch, the direction of movement depending upon the location of the holddown screw. Loosen the screw slightly and set the gap to compensate.

Condenser. Complete failure of the *condenser* will keep the engine from operating, its ignition current grounded through a shorted condenser or the point set burned to a nub by an open condenser. Most failures are partial: the engine may be hard to start, may misfire, or may develop a large appetite for point sets. Occa-

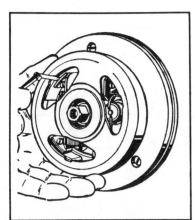

Fig. 7-30. The cam is integral with the flywheel on the Sachs and most other engines. Magneto adjustments are made through "windows" cut into the flywheel.

Table 7-2. Ignition System Specifications.

MAKE	POINT GAP	IGNITION ADVANCE BEFORE TDC	SPARKING GAP
Batavus M-48	0.35-0.45 mm (0.014-0.018 in.)	2.0-2.2 mm (0.079-0.087 in.)	0.016 in.
Velosolex	N.A.	N.A.	0.15-0.020 in.
Garelli			
Eureka, Katia Kick, KatiaM, Eureka Matic	0.30-0.50 mm (0.014-0-020 in.)	1.5 mm (0.059 in.)	0.020-0.024 in.
Fichtel & Sachs (engine)			
505/1A	0.35-0.45 mm (0.014-0.018 in.)	2.5-3.0 mm (0.098-0.118 in.)	0.020 in.
505/1ANL			
505/1B		see text for clarification	
505/1C			
Jawa	N.A.	1.5 mm (0.059 in.)	0.024 in.
Babetta			
Minarelli (engine)		1.67 mm (0.066 in.)	0.015 in.
V1	0.35-0.40 mm (0.014-0.018 in.)		
Motobecane all models	0.35-0.40 mm (0.014-0.018 in.)	N.A.	
Peugeot			
103 LS-U1, 103 LVS-U2, 103 LVS-U3	0.30-0.50 mm (0.012-0.020 in.)	1.5 mm (0.059 in.)	0.016 in.
Puch Maxi	0.40-0.50 mm (0.016-0.020 in.)	0.8-1.2 mm (0.031-0.047 in.)	0.020 in.
Tomas Automatic 3, A3	0.35-0.45 mm (0.014-0.018 in.)	1.8-2.0 mm (0.071-0.079 in.)	0.019 in.

sionally, a condenser will fail when hot, after a quarter hour or so of operation and, once cool, behave normally.

Condensers open, short, or change *capacitance*. Change in capacitance is a gradual process, caused by metal migration from one plate to the other or a deteriorating dielectric.

Opens and shorts can be detected by the device shown in Fig. 7-31. Power is supplied by the line cord; about 150 volts dc appears at the test clips. One clip is connected to the condenser case, the other to its lead. Reducing the value of the two 27-kilohm resistors makes the device more sensitive, but increases the hazard of electrical shock. At their present value, the output is less than lethal, although you should connect the clips *before* you plug the device in and leave the clips in place until you disconnect power. The 1 megohm resistor in parallel with the condenser is a discharge path for the condenser. If you take the condenser out of the circuit with power on, the condenser will "bite." Nothing lethal, but uncomfortable.

The condenser is serviceable if the neon bulb flickers once when power is connected. If the bulb does not react or if it continues to glow or blink, replace the condenser. Check the replacement before you install it; new condensers can also be faulty.

If you do not want to build or purchase a tester, the best course of action is to replace the condenser each time the points are serviced. The condenser is secured to the stator plate by a screw and strap arrangement. Remove the holddown screw (two on the Motobecane) and disconnect the lead between the condenser and the point set. On a few older mopeds, the condenser lead is soldered. Heat the connection and pull the wire free.

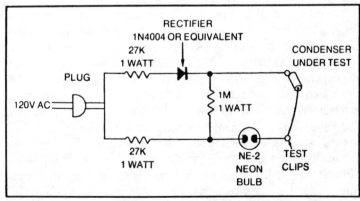

Fig. 7-31. Condenser checker. House the assembly in a clear plastic box.

Remove any oil accumulation under the mounting strap and install the replacement condenser. Snug the screw down tight, but not so tight that it pulls out the threads: remember, you are dealing with aluminum. Connect the lead to the point set. If the lead must be soldered, use a pencil-type gun and low-melting-point, rosin-core solder. Heat the connection until the solder melts and flows into the wires: too little heat leaves a lumpy, unreliable joint; too much can damage the condenser. However the wire is connected, check that it is routed away from the flywheel and the movable point arm.

Coils. *Exciter and ignition coils,* whether combined or in two separate units, are best tested by substitution. Generally, the exciter section fails first, for it is subject to engine heat and vibration.

External Circuit. Failure of the *external circuit* can also disable the ignition. Check the taillamp for continuity by disconnecting its lead and grounding it to the engine. If this solves the problem (the engine will run), the taillamp is burnt out or the taillamp ground is open. Take the kill switch out of the circuit by removing it physically from the handlebar. If the engine runs with the switch ungrounded, the difficulty is in the switch.

In rare instances, the spark plug cable or the radio suppressor fitted between the cable end and the spark plug may fail. Again, the best test is by means of substitution.

SOLID-STATE IGNITION

At present, Jawa's Tranzimo is the only solid-state ignition available on mopeds. The technology involved appears to be quite unsophisticated. A transistor replaces the contact points. Without points the engine should remain in time longer and tune-ups should be simpler. On the other hand, failure is absolute and unrepairable by the side of the road, unless you have a spare transistor.

Figure 7-32 illustrates the alternator, less the rotor. One coil, the uppermost in the drawing, generates power for ignition; the other three feed lights and accessories. The small coil on the stator plate is a trigger, generating a small command voltage for the transistor.

Figure 7-33 is a schematic of the circuit. The Tranzimo unit (2) houses the transistor and the secondary ignition coil. The transistor is connected to the primary ignition coil, the trigger coil, and the kill switch (8) on the handlebar. Internal connections are not shown, but a resistor is in series with the signal lead, and the output side of the transistor connects to the secondary coil. The rotor is keyed

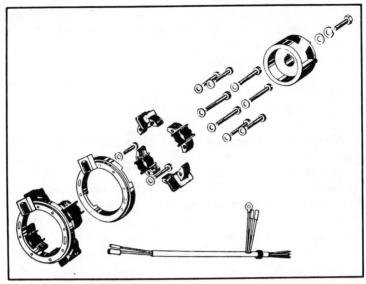

Fig. 7-32. The generating section of the Jawa Tranzimo. One large coil provides energy for the spark; the small coil atop the stator plate signals the transistor to conduct.

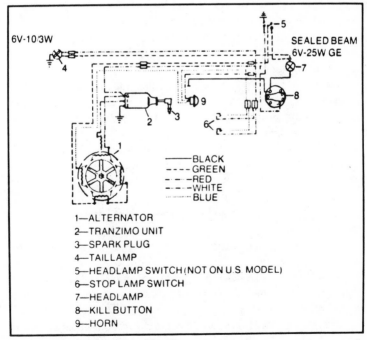

————BLACK
- - - - GREEN
- - —RED
- ·—WHITE
·········—BLUE

1—ALTERNATOR
2—TRANZIMO UNIT
3—SPARK PLUG
4—TAILLAMP
5—HEADLAMP SWITCH (NOT ON U.S. MODEL)
6—STOP LAMP SWITCH
7—HEADLAMP
8—KILL BUTTON
9—HORN

Fig. 7-33. The Tranzimo in schematic.

to the crankshaft and has permanent magnets in its rim. As the crank turns, one magnet generates voltage across the primary ignition coil. This voltage is blocked by the transistor until a second rotor magnet excites the trigger coil. The coil signals the transistor to conduct, and ignition voltage goes to the secondary ignition coil. There it is boosted to fire the spark plug.

Service

The following comments pertain to the Tranzimo, but can be applied to other makes.

Test the output as described under "Ignition System Troubleshooting." If the spark is weak, nonexistent, or erratic, begin with the obvious—the mechanical integrity of the generating section and its wiring. Remove the rotor cover and measure the clearance between the rotor and field coils. In the case of the Tranzimo, the specification is 0.012 inch. You can use a steel feeler gauge as long as you turn the rotor magnets away from the check points. Nonferrous gauges, used for air-conditioning clutch work, are available from auto supply houses, and give more consistent readings. If adjustment is necessary, loosen the coil holddown screws a few turns. The screws must be tight enough to hold the coils against the magnetic attraction of the rotor but not so tight that the coils cannot be gently tapped into place. Use a light hammer and a wooden dowel, positioning the dowel against the laminated iron coil shoes. Tighten the screws fully when clearance is correct.

Wear marks on the rotor edges, showing that the rotor has touched the coil shoes, mean that rotor-coil clearance is insufficient. This may be a simple matter of adjustment, or it may mean that the main bearings—the two bearings that support the crankshaft and the rotor—are worn. To determine if this is so, check the adjustment and then, using a socket wrench for purchase, bear down hard on the rotor (Fig. 7-34). If the rotor moves down into contact with the coil shoes, the main bearings are no longer up to the job of locating the crankshaft and should be replaced, together with the crankshaft seals.

Hard starting and misfiring at high speed can sometimes be corrected by withdrawing the rotor from the crankshaft and polishing the rotor magnets and coil shoes (Fig. 7-35). Use fine sandpaper to brighten these parts; a thin patina of rust is enough to scatter the magnetic fields.

The wiring should be tucked clear of the rotor, well out of harm's way, and soldered to the field coils. Trace the circuit out of the alter-

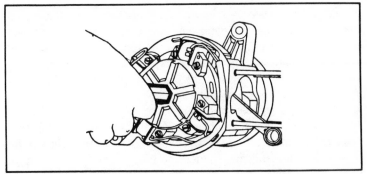

Fig. 7-34. Using a socket wrench for purchase, move the rotor up and down to detect main bearing wear.

nator and to the Tranzimo switching unit on the frame. Make and break the bayonet connectors several times to reestablish solid contact. Heavy corrosion can be removed with television tuner cleaner, available in aerosol cans from electronic parts houses and large hardware stores.

The Tranzimo switching unit has several features that are not found on other solid-state systems. The back of the unit is sealed with a Bakelite cap, reminiscent of the distributor cap on an automobile. Remove the cap and examine its inner and outer surfaces under a strong light. Not all defects are obvious to the eye; some appear like penciled marks on the cap. These carbon tracks glisten as the cap is turned under the light and mean that there is a current path between the high voltage terminal and ground. The path may be internal and hidden. When in doubt, replace the cap.

Another special feature of the Tranzimo is the external transistor, secured to the switching unit by its three soldered leads.

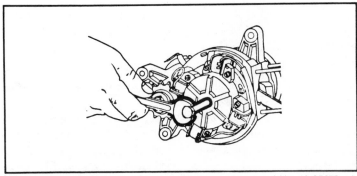

Fig. 7-35. Tranzimo rotor is extracted with Jawa special tool No. 16-65672-4.3.

Should the transistor fail, it will fail completely, like a light bulb. Test by substitution: unsolder the leads and, using a small, pencil-type iron, solder in a new transistor. Carefully note the lead connections, because a wiring error may destroy the new part. Use rosin-core solder and protect the transistor with a heat sink. Commercial heat sinks are available, or you can fabricate a substitute by wrapping a rubber band tightly around the jaws of a pair of needle-nosed pliers. The rubber band clamps the jaws together and the steel pliers absorb and dissipate heat. Position the heat sink between the transistor and the joint to be soldered.

If these gambles fail—and replacing the transistor and cap are gambles—then it is time to break out the voltmeter and do some serious troubleshooting. You must determine whether the fault is in the generating section or in one of the buried components of the switching circuit. The presence or absence of voltage is the diagnostic indicator.

The red wire is connected to one of the main generating coils and supplies current for the ignition pulse; the white wire is connected to the trigger coil and signals the transistor to conduct. Disconnect the red wire at the Tranzimo unit, and connect one probe of the voltmeter to it and the other to ground. Crank the engine to starting speed—the meter should show at least 40 volts ac. If it does not, replace the generating coil and recheck. Make the same test with the white wire, expecting to find no less than 3 volts between it and ground. In the unlikely event that the trigger coil is defective, replace it, together with the stator plate. These parts are not available separately.

Suppose that both voltages are within specification. What then? By elimination, the fault is somewhere inside the Tranzimo switching unit. Because the circuits are buried in epoxy, the whole unit must be replaced.

IGNITION TIMING

The ignition system determines when the spark occurs. On all gasoline engines, the moment of sparking occurs early, before the piston has reached top dead center. This allows time for the air/fuel mixture to ignite, burn, and generate pressure. By the time the piston has gone past top dead center, pressure is at its maximum.

While some ignition advance is needed, too much is deadly. The inertia of the flywheel and the forward motion of the machine send it toward the top of the bore. At the same time, the explosive forces above it attempt to send the piston down, reversing the engine. The piston does not suffer long—it simply melts.

If the spark occurs late, the brunt of combustion energy is lost against the already sinking piston: most of the energy escapes out the exhaust port. The engine may be difficult to start and, once started, will produce little power.

Moped timing is fixed; once set it remains at a specific advance regardless of engine speed or load. Some readers who are familiar with the centrifugal and vacuum advance mechanisms on automobiles may wonder about the advisability of fixed timing. Some performance is lost, because the time required for combustion is almost independent of piston speed. At high speed, a moped spark occurs late relative to peak combustion pressure. On the other hand, two-cycle engines are more tolerant of fixed timing than are four-cycle engines and will run slightly retarded without much fuss.

Ignition occurs at the precise moment the contact points separate on conventional systems. Breakerless systems fire when the trigger coil and sensing magnet are in opposition. The purpose of timing is to match the moment of firing with a specified position of the piston, expressed as millimeters of travel before top dead center.

There are several ways to determine when the points break. The most accurate method is to use a continuity lamp, a buzzer, or an *ohmmeter* (Fig. 7-36). Connect one test lead to the movable arm of the point set, the other to a good, paint-and-oil-free engine ground. Turn the flywheel in the direction of normal rotation and watch the lamp or meter. The lamp should dim, and the meter needle should drop as the points part. A more precise reading will re-

Fig. 7-36. This test lamp is available from Kohler under part No. 33-455-10.

Fig. 7-37. Minarelli engines have timing marks.

sult if you disconnect the lead between the point set and the exciter coil; the coil is grounded and alters the results a bit.

Another, less accurate way to determine when the points open is to place a piece of cellophane between the contacts and turn the wheel until the cellophane is released. This is an emergency procedure only, because the timing will be off by the thickness of the cellophane.

Tranzimo rotors and stator plates carry timing marks. When these marks are in line with each other, the unit fires.

With magneto or solid state systems, the moment of firing can be adjusted by turning the stator plate in its elongated mounting holes. Turning the plate against the direction of crankshaft rotation advances the timing; turning it with crankshaft rotation retards the timing. Magneto systems have a second variable—the point gap. The wider the gap, the earlier the contacts open, and the more advanced is the ignition. Narrowing the gap has the reverse effect, which is why gapping the points to specification can do wonders for engine power.

The moment of firing must be coordinated with piston movement. Minarelli engineers have simplified matters by providing timing marks on the flywheel (Fig. 7-37). The mark identified by the letter "A" is the timing mark; it is 23 degrees in advance of "0," or top dead center. Timing these engines is simple:

- Set the point gap to specification—0.35-0.40 mm (0.014-0.018 inch).
- Loosen the stator plate holddown screws so that the plate can be turned.
- Mount the flywheel, but do not thread on the nut.
- Hook up a lamp, or some other point-break indicator, with one lead on the movable point arm and the other lead grounded.
- Turn the flywheel in the direction of engine rotation—clockwise when facing the wheel—until the indicator shows point separation.
- If the "A" mark is not aligned with the pointer at the instant the points open, move the stator plate. Chances are the engine will not be far out of time and a few taps on the stator will be enough.
- Once you are satisfied that the "A" mark and point opening are synchronized, disconnect the timing indicator, tighten the stator plate holddown screws and assemble the flywheel and nut. There are no torque specs for this nut; the manufacturer assumes that you will use the stubby 15-mm wrench supplied with the bike which, because of its length, has a built-in torque limit.

Flywheel marks are convenient, but not entirely accurate. Most manufacturers prefer to specify timing directly from piston position. Timing becomes a matter of measurement, although there is a compromise available, represented by factory tools indexed for specific mopeds. The Motobecane is bottomed in the spark plug port and the flywheel turned against normal rotation. When the advance is correct the tool registers it.

The classic timing drill is more demanding; it begins with the search for true top dead center. You can use a plunger, like the one shown in Fig. 7-38 or a dial indicator. The latter is the more precise instrument, with scale divisions of 0.01 mm. Several engine manufacturers offer mounting fixtures—bosses that thread into the spark plug port, with or without the dial indicator. Kohler, Suzuki, and Yamaha offer the complete kit (Fig. 7-39) under parts numbers

Fig. 7-38. A timing plunger is an alternative to a dial indicator, although an inferior one.

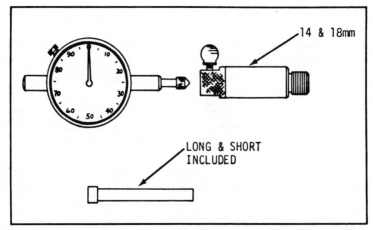

Fig. 7-39. This dial indicator and adapter kit is available from several manufacturers.

33 755 03, 09931 00111, and 908 90030 02 00, respectively. The spark plug port adapter is available from Puch as part number 905 6 32 101 0.

To time the engine with a dial indicator, gap the points to specification and follow this procedure:

● Mount the indicator on the cylinder head, threading it solidly into the spark plug port.

● Find top dead center by *bracketing*: move the crankshaft back and forth in progressively smaller increments.

● Once you are satisfied that the piston is at its high point, set the dial indicator at zero.

● Connect an ohmmeter or test lamp to the points.

● Determine the engine advance from Table 7-2 or by consultation with the dealer.

● Turn the crankshaft against normal rotation to a point well beyond advance specification.

● Turn the shaft in the direction of engine rotation to bring the piston to the advance specification. The points should just crack open.

If they don't, move the stator plate so they do, and tighten the hold-down screws.

Most Fichtel & Sachs engines have timing marks on the flywheel and crankcase. "0" represents top dead center and "M" is the firing mark. Some engines have come off the line without these marks, however, and it is necessary to make them:

- Find top dead center as before.
- Mark the flywheel and crankcase at some visible spot to indicate TDC.
- Turn the crankshaft against the direction of rotation. The spark advance on this engine is 2.5—3.0 mm. *Translated by the angle of the spark plug port this dimension is 3.5—4.0 mm (0.138-0.165 inch).*
- Indicate this advance on the flywheel, adjacent to the previously made crankcase mark.
- Gap the points at 0.35—0.45 mm (0.014—0.018 inch).
- As described earlier, move the stator plate so that the points break with the flywheel firing and crankcase reference marks aligned.

Peugeot magnetos employ a rotor that is free to move relative to the crankshaft. This changes the timing procedure somewhat. On other magnetos you can disregard the position of the flywheel magnetos, since they are part of the wheel and keyed to the crankshaft. Follow this procedure with Peugeot engines:

- Find true top dead center as before.
- Turn the crankshaft (by means of the clutch drum) to bring the piston well in advance of top dead center.
- Turn the drum to bring the piston 1.5 mm before top dead center.
- Without moving the crankshaft, turn the rotor to align its timing mark "2" with the "1" mark on the stator.
- Secure the rotor with Peugeot special tool No. 69646 or a pin wrench adapted to fit the holes.
- The rotor is secured by a 16 mm capscrew. Torque it to 18 ft-lb.
- Recheck the timing marks to be sure they have not slipped out of alignment.
- Loosen the point holddown screw a bit. Insert a screwdriver blade in the adjusting slot on the stationary point assembly.
- Adjust the gap until the points crack open. Tighten the hold-down screw and recheck.

The nominal point gap is 0.40 mm (0.016 in.), but this consideration is secondary to the need for accurate timing. So long as the gap falls between 0.30 and 0.50 mm (0.012—0.020 inch), the magneto will function.

LIGHTING CIRCUITS

Mopeds use 6-volt lighting systems. Three coils in the Tranzimo unit provide energy for the lights and horn; conventional magneto systems employ a single lighting coil for the headlamp and use the exciter to operate tail and brake lamps. The coils and magnets that generate energy for the system are known collectively as the *alternator*. Because the Tranzimo alternator is distinct from the ignition section (sharing only the rotor magnets), it has few problems for the serviceman. Magneto systems are another matter.

MAGNETO CIRCUITS

Figure 7-40 is a typical schematic. One side of the exciter is

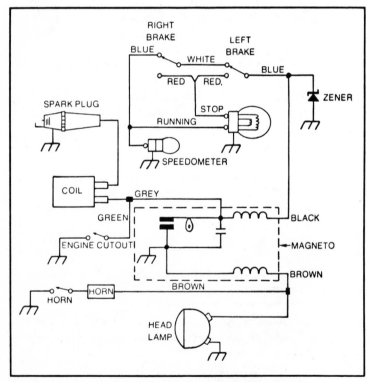

Fig. 7-40. A typical (magneto-fired) lighting and ignition system.

grounded when the contact points close; the other side is connected to the black wire, which joins the blue wire at a point near the handlebars. Both left and right brake levers incorporate stop-lamp switches; tripping either one operates the stop filament in the taillamp by way of the red wires. The blue wire continues through the tandem switches and provides power for the running filament.

Ignition Ground

Both the stop and running filaments are grounded at the lamp and provide a ground return for the ignition circuit. Current generated in the exciter flows through the closed points to ground and completes its circuit at the taillamp. As long as this circuit is completed, there is ignition voltage. If either of the taillamp filaments open, there will be trouble. A broken or burned out stop filament will disable the ignition *when* the brakes are engaged; a broken running filament will disable the ignition *unless* the brakes are engaged.

Circuit Refinements

The *zener diode* in the upper right-hand corner of Fig. 7-40 limits voltage to the taillamp. The lamp is rated at 6 volts, a much lower voltage than the exciter coil delivers at high rpm. The zener "spills" the additional voltage to ground, protecting the lamp filaments. Should the zener short, all exciter current goes to ground, and there is no voltage available for the lamp or for the ignition coil. Should the zener open—the usual mode of failure—the taillamp burns out as soon as the throttle is opened.

In order to meet U.S. Department of Transportation standards, mopeds must be electrically clean; that is, the ignition system cannot transmit signals that interfere with radio and television reception. Most manufacturers meet this requirement by incorporating a resistor in the spark plug cable, usually at the terminal.

Peugeot has a fairly unique system: high-frequency oscillations, the oscillations that produce pips on TV screens and static in radio sets, are dampened by means of a *choke*, or *reactance coil* (Fig. 7-41). This coil has little effect on low-frequency oscillations. The current produced by the exciter coil alternates: it moves to-and-fro in the circuit, peaking in one direction, falling to zero, and peaking in the other. The rectifier is a kind of traffic cop: it blocks half of the alternations to keep electrical traffic moving in one direction. Without it, exciter output would short to ground through the reactance coil,

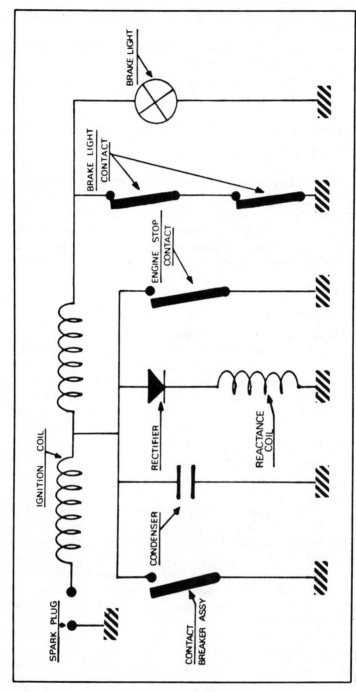

Fig. 7-41. The Peugeot ignition and tail lamp circuit features a rectifier and reactance coil.

and there would be no ignition. Should the rectifier open, the circuit will continue to function, although it will radiate interference. Your TV-watching neighbors will know when you ride by.

Another interesting feature of the Peugeot circuit is that the stop lamp switches are connected in series and normally grounded. Because the resistance of the switch contacts is lower than the resistance of the stop lamp filament, no current passes through the filament unless one or both switches are opened. Any condition that denies ground will affect operation. For example, if the switch contacts are dirty, the stop lamp will burn continuously; if the stop lamp burns out, the engine will stop when the brakes are applied; if there is a break in the wire ahead of the switches, the engine will not run at all.

The usual European practice is to stop the engine with a compression release (Fig. 7-42). To meet American standards, manufacturers have added and, in some cases, substituted, a kill switch on the right handlebar. The kill switch is shown in Figs. 7-40 and 7-41. It is a simple grounding switch, wired to the ignition-coil side of the exciter. A mechanic should remember that a faulty kill switch can disable the ignition.

REPAIRS

Once the trouble is spotted, electrical repairs are simple. Most involve defective grounds caused by rust, oil, or paint at the connections. Scrape the connections down to bare metal and make certain that they are secured by holddown screws or, in the case of lamp sockets, by spring pressure. The insulated side of the circuit usually fails because of dirty connections or broken wires. The most vulnerable wiring runs under the rear fender to feed the taillights.

Broken wires, or wires that have lost their insulation and short, can be replaced on a one-to-one basis. You can open the wiring harness, cut out the faulty wiring, and splice in new lengths. Use stranded wire, known in the automotive trades as *primary wire*, of at least the same gauge (thickness) as the original.

Mopeds generally use No. 16 or slightly heavier No. 14 wire. Hair-thin 20-gauge wire is sometimes used at the instrument nacelle. Remember, you can always go to heavier wire, but you're asking for trouble if you use thinner. Also remember that gauge number and thickness are inversely related: the higher the number, the thinner the wire (and the less current it will safely carry).

The nice thing about the electrical system is that many

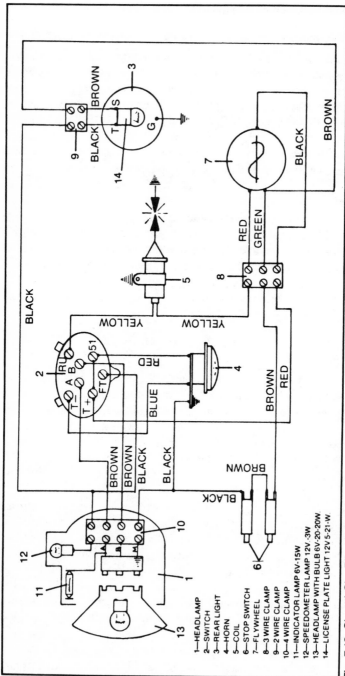

Fig. 7-42. Cimatti City Bike wiring diagram (U.S. version).

1—HEADLAMP
2—SWITCH
3—REAR LIGHT
4—HORN
5—COIL
6—STOP SWITCH
7—FLYWHEEL
8—3 WIRE CLAMP
9—2 WIRE CLAMP
10—4 WIRE CLAMP
11—INDICATOR LAMP 6V-15W
12—SPEEDOMETER LAMP 12V-3W
13—HEADLAMP WITH BULB 6V-20-20W
14—LICENSE PLATE LIGHT 12V 5-21-W.

components—wire, connections, switches, lamp sockets—can be purchased from nondealer sources. Six-volt sealed-beam headlamps are a standard item, used on small tractors and riding mowers. The quality of these parts is at least as good as those the factory supplies and the cost is less.

On the other hand, some electrical components are specific to mopeds. Taillamp bulbs are a good example—automotive bulbs draw too much current and, at any rate, do not have the reinforced filaments necessary to withstand motorbike vibration. And be careful about making modifications. A motorcycle horn—one that motorists can actually hear-may seem like a good idea, but moped alternators do not have power to spare, and the horn could burn out a coil.

Chapter 8

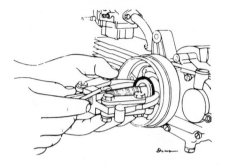

The Engine

Moped engines are rather complex (Fig. 8-1 through 8-4); major disassembly should not be entered into lightly. If you do decide to open the engine, go about the work in an orderly, patient manner with clean tools and hands. If the parts can be assembled wrong—some cylinder heads, for example, can go on three wrong ways and one right way—mark them while they are still together. The piston is critical; it can be installed 180 degrees off unless you take notice of the factory mark or, if that mark is missing, make your own.

Another difficulty is that some manufacturers have not developed torque limit specifications, expecting that dealer mechanics develop a feel for these things. Torque limits that are available are included in Table 8-1, standard torque limits by bolt and screw size are in Table 8-2. The first table was compiled from factory manuals and has precedence over the second table. Both tables assume that the fastener threads are in good condition and are lubricated with clean motor oil.

DURABILITY

How long do moped engines last? The manufacturers are not saying, and few dealers have the experience to make more than a guess. Small motorcycles are superficially similar to mopeds; some of them are made by the same factories. These machines are not durable—the Department of Transportation is satisfied if they hold together for 20,000 miles—nor are they repairable in any true sense

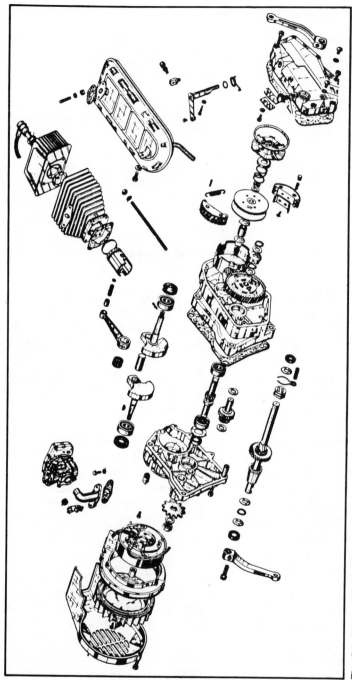

Fig. 8-1. Minarelli V1 engine.

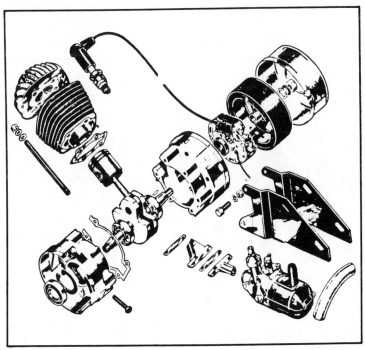

Fig. 8-2. Batavus (Laura) M48.01 engine.

of the word. As mechanics say, "it's one ring job between the showroom floor and the junkyard."

Mopeds are different from motorcycles in concept, in market potential, and in purpose. Motorcycles, even the smallest of them, are leisure products sold on the promise of performance. Performance—and some 50 cc. motorcycle engines can deliver upwards of 12-hp—is almost always gained at the expense of longevity. In contrast, mopeds are designed under legal restrictions that limit power and top speed. Moped engines are detuned for the European market and further detuned to meet American regulations. Few of them turn more than 5000 rpm and some develop no more than a hair over 1 hp.

Mopeds were originally intended as transportation for the working people of Europe, who insisted upon durability and, when something finally broke, repairability. While any small engine is a precision product, moped engines carry precision to a degree unknown elsewhere. No machine tool turns out identical parts; there is always some variation from the blueprint specifications. Moped builders compensate for this by grading and matching parts accor-

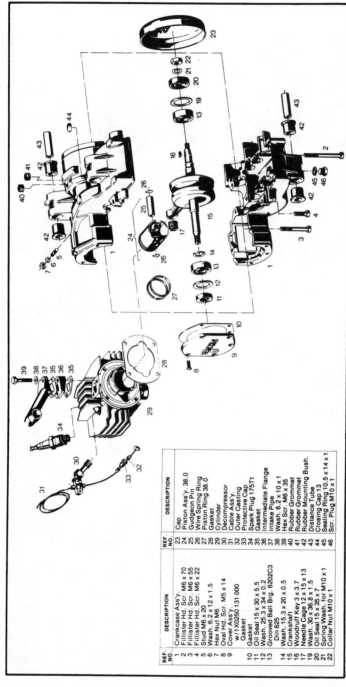

REF. NO.	DESCRIPTION		REF. NO.	DESCRIPTION
1	Crankcase Ass'y.		23	Cap
2	Fillister Hd. Scr. M6 x 70		24	Piston Ass'y. 38.0
3	Fillister Hd. Scr. M6 x 55		25	Gudgeon Pin
4	Fillister Hd. Scr. M6 x 22		26	Wire Spring Ring
5	Stud M6 x 20		27	Piston Ring 38.0
6	Wash. 6.2 x 12 x 1.5		28	Gasket
7	Hex Nut M6		29	Cylinder
8	Oval Hd. Scr. M5 x 14		30	Decompressor
9	Cover Ass'y.		31	Cable Ass'y.
	w/1X0250 131 000		32	Outer Casting
10	Gasket		33	Protective Cap
11	Oil Seal 15 x 30 x 5.5		34	Spark Plug 175T1
12	Wash. 25.3 x 34 x 0.2		35	Gasket
13	Grooved Ball Brg. 6202C3		36	Intermediate Flange
	Din 625		37	Intake Pipe
14	Wash. 15.3 x 20 x 0.5		38	Wash. 6.2 x 10 x 1
15	Crankshaft		39	Hex Scr. M6 X 35
16	Woodruff Key 3 x 3.7		40	Rubber Grommet
17	Needle Cage 12 x 15 x 13		41	Rubber Grommet
18	Wash. 30 x 36.8 x 1.5		42	Rubber Mounting Bush.
19	Oil Seal 15 x 35 x 7		43	Distance Tube
20	Oil Seal 15 x 35 x 7		44	Closing Cap 13
21	Spring Wash. for M10 x 1		45	Sealing Ring 10.5 x 14 x 1
22	Collar Nut M10 x 1		46	Scr. Plug M10 x 1

Fig. 8-3. Fichtel & Sachs 505/1A engine. Courtesy Columbia Mfg. Co.

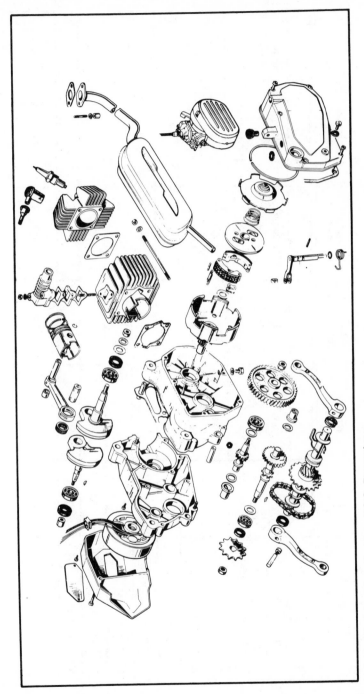

Fig. 8-4. Morini engine. Courtesy F.G.S. Enterprises.

Table 8-1. Torque Limits by Manufacturer.

Make	Cylinder Head	Cylinder Barrel	Crankcase Fasteners	Flywheel Nut	Clutch Nut (Engine)	Motor Mount
Batavuus M-48						
Garelli	1.8 kgm (17.9Nm) (13.0 ft-lb)	NA / NA	0.9kgm (8.8Nm) (6.5 ft-lb)	3.3kgm (32.4Nm) (24.0 ft-lb)	3.5kgm (34.3Nm) (25.3 ft-lb)	NA / NA
Eureka, Katia Kick Katio M, Eureka Matic						
Fitchtel & Sachs (engine)	NA	(0.8-1.0 kgm) (7.8-9.8Nm) 5.7-7.2 ft-lb	(1-1.2 kgm) (9.8-11.8 Nm) 7.2-8.7 ft-lb	3.7-4 kgm 36.3-39.2Nm 26.7-28.9 ft-lb	(3.5-4.0 kgm) 3.6-3.9Nm 25.3-28.9 ft-lb	NA
Jawa						
Babetta	NA	NA	NA	NA	NA	NA
Minarelli (engine)						
all models	NA	NA	NA	NA	NA	NA
Motobecane						
all models	NA	NA	NA	NA	NA	NA

Model					
Peugeot 103 LS-U1, 103 VLS-U2, 103 LVS-U3	1.1kmg (10.8Nm) (7.9 ft-lb)	NA NA NA	see note 1 see note 1 see note 1	4.0kgm (39.2Nm) (29.0 ft-lb)	4.0kgm (39.2Nm) (29.0 ft-lb) / 2.5kgm (24.5Nm) (18.0 ft-lb)
Puch Maxi	1.0kgm (10.0Nm) (7.3 ft-lb)	1.0kgm 10Nm 7.3 ft-lb	2.7kgm (27Nm) (19.5 ft-lb)	3.5 kgm (35Nm) (25.4 ft-lb)	0.8kgm (8Nm) (5.8 ft-lb)
Tomas Automatic 3	1.2kgm (11.8Nm) (8.7 ft-lb)	NA NA NA	1.0kgm (11.7Nm) (7.2 ft-lb)	3.0 kgm (29.4Nm) (21.7 ft-lb)	NA NA NA
Velosolex	1.2kgm 11.5Nm 8.5 ft-lb	0.8kgm 8.2Nm 6.1 ft-lb	0.8 kgm 7.4Nm 5.4 ft lb	3.3 kgm 32.1Hm 23.7 ft-lb	NA NA see chapter 7 / NA NA NA see note 2

Note 1: Peugeot crankcases are held together by six bolts, five are torqued to 0.9 kgm (8.83 nm. 6.5 ft-lb); the remaining bolt is torqued 1.2 kgm (11.8 nm, 8.7 ft-lb).

Note 2: Velosolex engine mount torque limits are in inch-pounds divide by 12 for foot-pounds.

1.2 kgm
0.9 kgm
0.9 kgm   0.9 kgm
0.9 kgm
0.9 kgm

97   162   73
65
65
65
73

139

Table 8-2. Torque Limits by Bolt Size.

Unit: kgm (lbs-ft)

Part	Torque
6 mm screw	0.7 — 1.0(5.1 — 7.2)
6 mm hex bolt	0.8 — 1.2(5.8 — 8.7)
8 mm hex bolt	1.8 — 2.5(13.0 — 18.1)
10 mm hex bolt	3.0 — 4.0(21.7 — 28.9)
6 mm flanged hex bolt	1.0 — 1.4(7.2 — 10.1)
8 mm flanged hex bolt	2.4 — 3.0(17.4 — 21.7)
10 mm flanged hex bolt	3.8 — 4.8(27.5 — 34.7)

ding to size. Most have three grades of cylinder bores and pistons, so that larger-than-average pistons can service larger-than-average bores. Some have as many as eight grades. This concern with precise fit makes inventory problems, but it does much to assure that the engine will live a long useful life.

Under-stressing the engine and extreme care in assembly has paid off. Robert E. Drennan is vice-president for customer service at Cimatti, and his comments are typical of what one hears in the industry. Cimatti and several other bikes use the Minarelli engine. Drennan reports that he has never seen a worn-out Minarelli, even though he has inspected scores of them that are used in rental service on East Coast beachfronts.

Reliability—the freedom from sudden, unexpected mechanical catastrophe—appears to be good. Reliability comes about because of the low power outputs and because of the design stability of these machines. Many of the better known mopeds were designed 20 years ago, and some date back before World War II. Newcomers are usually quite conservative, sometimes going so far as to copy existing designs.

CYLINDER HEAD

About half of the mopeds presently imported have detachable cylinder heads (Fig. 8-5); the others have the head and cylinder barrel cast as one unit. Comments about compression release valves, decarbonizing, and polishing apply to all engines. Those with one-piece heads and cylinders must have their barrels removed for access.

Mark the cylinder head and barrel before disassembly, because on many engines the head bolts are spaced evenly, and the head

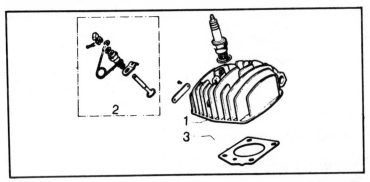

Fig. 8-5. Motobecane cylinder head (1), gasket (3), and compression release (2).

can be installed three ways wrong and one way right. Remove the spark plug and, if present, the compression release control cable. Undo the four cap screws securing the head to the barrel, noting the washer under each screw. Lift the head off.

Compression Release

The *compression release* is a small poppet valve, not unlike those used on four-cycle engines. It is opened by a cable-and-lever arrangement and closed by spring tension. After long service, the valve may fail to seat, leaking compression through the port drilled through the head and barrel. Test the valve by covering its face with soap suds and introducing compressed air at the port. Bubbles mean the valve should be disassembled for cleaning.

The pin that holds the valve on the spring collar is as important as any part on the bike. If it should fail, the valve can fall into the cylinder and break the piston. As shown in Fig. 8-5, Motobecane compression releases are fixed by a cotter pin; Peugeot valves are secured by a brass rod, peened over the ends. Other makes use a spring clip. Release the locking mechanism and pull the valve out of the cylinder. Normally, all that is required is to wire brush the valve face and seat.

If the valve appears burnt or warped, it can be resurfaced by lapping, but the job is a little tricky. The valve must be turned against its seat. One way to do this is to glue a small-diameter dowel to the valve head, securing it with potent adhesive such as alpha-cyano-acrylic cement. Dab a little lapping compound on the seat and rotate the valve between the palms of your hands. After a few seconds the compound will pulverize and you will no longer hear the "swish-swish" sound of it cutting. Raise the valve, wipe off the

141

Fig. 8-6. Hold the head in a vise by the bolts. Copper plate on the jaws will protect the bolt threads.

exhausted compound, and add more. Repeat the operation until the full circumference of the valve and seat are uniformly bright. Take special care to remove all the compound; it must not get into the engine.

In the unlikely event that the whole assembly must be replaced, secure the head in a vise, as shown in Fig. 8-6, covering the vise jaws with copper sheet to protect the bolt threads. Unscrew the valve body.

Decarbonizing

Even a thin layer of carbon costs power; thick layers send the engine into detonation. Scrape the cylinder head and piston top with a dull knife, trying not to mar the machined surfaces. Nicks and gouges are the sign of amateur work and make the next decarbonizing job more difficult. Move the piston down into the bore and wipe off any loose carbon flakes on the cylinder walls.

Cylinder Head Truing

This step is optional on engines that have not had a history of head-gasket problems. Secure a piece of plate glass—ordinary window glass will not do—to a flat surface and coat it with valve-lapping compound. Place the head, gasket surface down, on the glass and move it in a figure-8 pattern (Fig. 8-7). Your hand should be centered on the head so the whole gasket surface should be uniformly bright. Continue lapping until any low spots disappear.

Note that this operation is not the same as milling or grinding the head. Moped cylinder heads will not tolerate much metal removal before the compression ratio goes out of sight or the *squish band*, the indentation around the edge of the chamber, is lost. Lapping is a finishing operation that takes off no more than a few thousandths of an inch.

Fig. 8-7. Surfacing a Batavus cylinder head.

Increased efficiency will result if you polish the combustion chamber and piston top (*not* the gasket surface). Engines have been polished by hand, although the job goes much faster with a high-speed drill motor. Begin with a wire cup brush and progress to finer and finer grades of wet-or-dry sandpaper. Oil speeds the cutting and leaves a smoother surface. After about grade 400, use a buffer and jeweler's rouge. The job is done when you can see your reflection.

Head Gasket

Most engines use a composition gasket that must be replaced each time the head is disturbed: to do otherwise is to ask for leaks. A few mopeds use copper gaskets that can be reused if the gasket is heated with a propane torch and quenched in water. Puch engines employ spacers made of heavy gauge aluminum foil. These spacers are one of the factory tricks to detune the engine for the American market. If you wish, they can be discarded. Seal the head and barrel with a very thin coat of high-temperature silicon cement.

Assembly

Mount the head on the barrel, making sure that the gasket and head are aligned with each other and with the reference marks previously made. Inspect the head bolts for straightness and, particularly, for evidence of thread damage. Lubricate the bolt threads and cap undersides with motor oil or anti-sieze compound.

Run the bolts in until snug. Then, using a torque wrench, tighten the bolts in a diagonal pattern in at least three increments—one-third, two-thirds, and full torque. Torque limit specifications are in Table 8-1. Install the spark plug and compression-release cable.

CYLINDER BARREL

Most machines are constructed so the cylinder barrel can be detached with the engine in place. French belt-drive machines are an exception; the engine must be dropped for cylinder clearance. (Peugeot cylinders can be removed with the engine in the frame if you have special tool No. 69260, a belt-pulley spring compressor.)

The barrel, or *jug*, is secured to the crankcase by four capscrews or studs. The studs may double as cylinder-head fasteners. Disconnect the exhaust pipe at the cylinder port and loosen the muffler brackets enough to swing the pipe clear. Disconnect the intake pipe or carburetor, whichever is easier. Undo the capscrews or studnuts in crisscross fashion in order to protect the cylinder bore from distortion. Lift the barrel far enough to see the piston, turn the crankshaft so the piston is at bottom dead center, and pull the barrel off (Fig. 8-8). If the piston were extended, it would drop hard against the crankcase.

It is not unusual for the barrel to be stubborn. Unseat it with a rubber mallet, directing the blows against the exhaust port outlet. Do not pound on the fins, which are glass-fragile on some models. Once the barrel is off, scrape the gasket remains from both parting surfaces.

Inspection

Wipe the bore with a clean shop towel and turn it under a strong light. The bore should be uniformly bright and smooth. The various sorts of damage and possible causes are:

- Discoloration—local overheating and distortion.
- Deep grooves running the length of the bore—piston ring

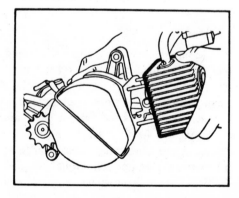

Fig. 8-8. Removing the cylinder barrel on a Jawa engine.

or bearing particle damage. Replace or, if possible, remachine the bore.

● Scratches at the exhaust port—carbon damage, a fact of life of two-cycle engines.

● Fine, almost invisible, scratches—sand damage. Check the air filter and intake tract joints.

● Peeling or worn-through chrome—manufacturing error or extreme wear. Replace.

● Aluminum splatter—piston damage. Remove the aluminum with muriatic (hydrochloric) acid. Flush with water and immediately oil the bore.

Once you are satisfied that the bore has no obvious defects, have it measured with a bore gauge or inside micrometer. The measuring points are shown in Fig. 8-9. Each point is measured twice, parallel with the wrist pin centerline and at 90 degrees to it.

At this juncture, things begin to get complicated. Moped engines are put together like a fine watch, from parts that are coded for size. Each size code has a wear limit, different for each manufacturer. For example, Puch uses five cylinder bore and piston sizes on the Maxi engine. Permissible out-of-round is 0.00098 in. (0.025 mm) in all cases, but there are five wear limits, varying with the original size of the cylinder. Table 8-3 lists cylinder and piston dimensions for the Maxi engine. Other manufacturers use a different cylinder bore base dimension or grade at different size intervals. At any rate,

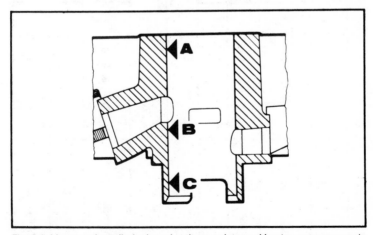

Fig. 8-9. Measure the cylinder barrel at these points, making two measurements parallel with the wrist pin and 180 degrees apart at each point. Courtesy Steyr-Daimler-Puch of America Corp.

Table 8-3. Puch Cylinder/Piston Tolerances.

Cylinder

	Tolerance 10 inch / mm	Tolerance 20 inch / mm	Tolerance 30 inch / mm	Tolerance 40 inch / mm	Tolerance 50 inch / mm
inch	1.4950 - 1.4954	1.4954 - 1.4958	1.4958 - 1.4962	1.4962 - 1.4966	1.4966 - 1.4970
mm	37.975 - 37.985	37.985 - 37.995	37.995 - 38.005	38.005 - 38.015	38.015 - 38.025

Piston

	Tolerance 10 inch / mm	Tolerance 20 inch / mm	Tolerance 30 inch / mm	Tolerance 40 inch / mm	Tolerance 50 inch / mm
inch	1.4938 - 1.4942	1.4942 - 1.4946	1.4946 - 1.4950	1.4950 - 1.4954	1.4954 - 1.4958
mm	37.945 - 37.955	37.955 - 37.965	37.965 - 37.975	37.975 - 37.985	37.985 - 37.995

Permissible ovality of the cylinder 0.00098 in. (0.025 mm)

the code will be stamped on the cylinder barrel, usually on the top fin, and the same code number or letter will appear on the piston crown.

Most moped engines have chromed bores. These bores last longer than plain iron, but complicate matters when they do finally wear out. It is impractical to machine a chrome bore to fit a larger piston. Should the bore be worn past specification, you have two choices: you can purchase a new cylinder and coded piston, or you can try to find a piston from one of the larger codes that will restore the fit. If, in the case of the Puch, your machine has a code 5 bore, oversize pistons are not to be had.

Honing

Cast-iron cylinders should be lightly honed before assembly (Fig. 8-10). (This process would be disastrous on chromed liners). Hon-

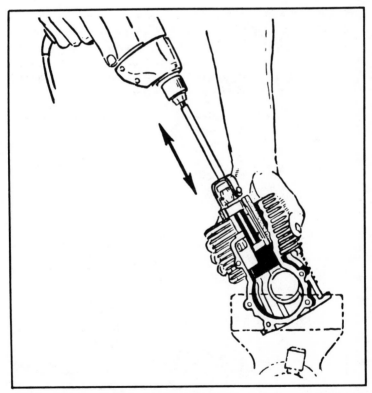

Fig. 8-10. Honing a cylinder—an operation that is limited to cast iron bores. Courtesy Clinton Engines Corp.

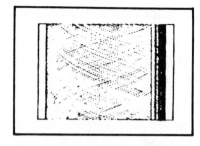

Fig. 8-11. The hone should leave a cross-hatch pattern, with diamond-shaped high spots between the abrasions. Courtesy Clinton Engines Corp.

ing removes small imperfections and leaves a regular pattern of scratches on the bore that help the rings seat (Fig. 8-11). Without honing, it is doubtful that chrome-plated rings would ever make a gas-tight seal.

Bona fide engine hones are not available in capacities of less than 2.00 inches. You must therefore use a heavy-duty brake cylinder hone. Hones with three stones, such as the Snap-on B-200, give more consistent results than two-stone models. Mount the hone in a low-speed drill motor, lubricate the cylinder with kerosene or cutting oil, and run the hone up and down in the bore. Adjust the reciprocating speed to give a cross-hatch pattern as shown in the illustration. The exact angle is not important—manufacturers specify anything from 22.5 to 60 degrees—what is important is that the pat-

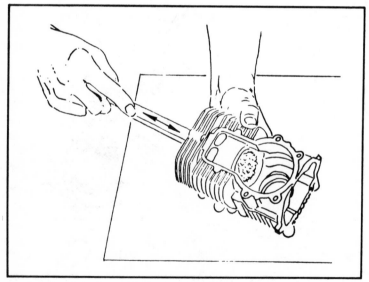

Fig. 8-12. Scrub the bore with hot water and detergent to remove the stone particles. Dry with paper towels and oil immediately. Courtesy Clinton Engines Corp.

tern have a definite diamond shape. Keep the hone moving, pausing at the end of the stroke only long enough to reverse direction. Stop when the glaze on the cylinder wall is broken. As a practical matter, some patches of glaze may be left, if removing them costs too much metal.

Once the cylinder is honed, scrub the bore with hot water and detergent (Fig. 8-12). Wipe with a paper towel; if the towel discolors, scrub again to float out the remaining abrasive particles. Lightly oil the cylinder to prevent rust.

Reboring

Most cast-iron cylinders can be rebored. Because cylinders retail for between $40 and $50, reboring is certainly worthwhile. The first step is to measure the cylinder accurately to determine how much metal must be taken out. Then purchase a piston in that oversize. The only real complication arises with engines that use tolerance-coded cylinder/piston assemblies. Jawa is a good example of this practice (see Table 8-4).

Jawa cylinder/piston combinations are supplied in four tolerances. Standard is unmarked; the remaining three are identified by a letter code stamped on the cylinder and piston. Each of these four combinations can be rebored in four quarter-millimeter increments; dealers stock 16 different pistons for this engine. The

Table 8-4. Jawa Babetta Rebore Limits by Cylinder/Piston Grades.

Diameter × H6		A	B	C
Standard	39.00 + 0.016	39.00 + 0.006	39.006 + 0.005	39.011 + 0.005
Rebore I	39.25 + 0.016	39.25 + 0.006	39.256 + 0.005	39.261 + 0.005
Rebore II	39.50 + 0.016	39.50 + 0.006	39.506 + 0.005	39.511 + 0.005
Rebore III	39.75 + 0.016	39.75 + 0.006	39.756 + 0.005	39.761 + 0.005
Rebore IV	40.00 + 0.016	40.00 + 0.006	40.006 + 0.005	40.011 + 0.005

Piston Grading (mm)

Piston Grading		A	B	C
Rebore I	39.116 − 0.006	39.106 − 0.006	39.111 − 0.005	39.116 − 0.005
Rebore II	39.366 − 0.016	39.356 − 0.006	39.361 − 0.005	39.366 − 0.005
Rebore III	39.616 − 0.016	39.606 − 0.006	39.611 − 0.005	39.616 − 0.005
Rebore IV	39.866 − 0.016	39.856 − 0.006	39.861 − 0.005	39.866 − 0.005

Yugoslavian Tomas is built on two tolerance codes, A and B. Each can be overbored a half millimeter.

Boring engines and the all-critical matter of piston fitting is best left to the expert. There are occasions when this is impractical, however, and some discussion of the process is in order. There are two ways to bore a cylinder—with a *boring bar* or with a hone. The former is preferable, since it is faster and more accurate. Cylinders with liners that extend below the fins can be mounted in a standard three-jaw lathe chuck. Those that must be held by the fins require a four-jaw chuck for centering. The cylinder is spun and the boring bar, a heavy bar with a carbide cutter, is fixed to the tailstock. Bore undersize first, then bring the cylinder out to specification with a hone.

The second method of boring a cylinder is to use a coarse hone. The process is similar to glaze breaking, but is carried further. The drill motor should turn at about 600 rpm, and the hone should be reciprocated about 40 strokes a minute. Run the stones clear of both ends of the bore for approximately 0.5 in. You will know when the bore is straight by the steady whine of the drill motor. If the motor bogs down on part of the stroke, that section of the bore is narrow and you should concentrate on it. Keep the stones well lubricated and clean them before abrasive particles scratch the bore. Continually monitor your progress with an inside micrometer or a cylinder gauge. As you approach the limit, change to a medium stone. Finally, chamber the port edges to prevent ring snag and scrub the bore with detergent and water.

Assembly

Position a new base gasket on the engine block, aligning it with the transfer port indentations. Some mechanics like to coat both sides of the gasket with a cellophane-thin layer of silicone adhesive. Turn the crankshaft to bring the piston clear of the block and insert a wooden wedge under it (Fig. 8-13). The wedge is a third hand,

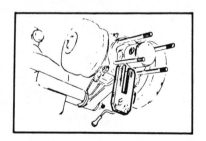

Fig. 8-13. A wedge under the piston simplifies barrel installation.

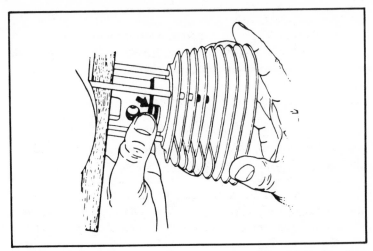

Fig. 8-14. The sleeve cutouts on Batavus and most other engines are a last-chance opportunity to compress the rings before they meet the bore.

holding the piston steady while you manipulate the cylinder barrel. Make certain that the piston rings are installed with their ends straddling the locating pins: if the closed section of a ring rides over the pin, the ring will snap when the barrel is lowered.

Lubricate the piston, rings, and wrist pin. Do the same for the cylinder bore, swabbing oil over every square millimeter of it. Turn the exhaust port down (or, as the case may be, forward) and lower the cylinder barrel. Do not turn it once you contact the piston; angular displacement can send the top compression ring over its locating pin. Gently push the barrel down, (Fig. 8-14) compressing the rings on the chamfer at the base of the bore. (Sachs engines are not chamfered and great care must be exercised not to break a ring.) If the barrel binds, stop and find out why. Once the piston is swallowed, lightly run in the barrel holddown fasteners. Turn the flywheel to detect possible "hard spots."

Torque the cylinder fasteners in several increments, working diagonally across the bore centerline. Mount the exhaust pipe and intake hardware.

PISTON

Examine the piston for heat damage, wear, and distortion. Combustion heat damage starts on the piston crown, or top. Before a hole develops, the metal rises and pits, as if it had been brought to a boil and cooled. Overheating on the cylinder bore sears and

151

blackens the piston skirts, sometimes ripping metal off in splotches. Discard a piston with either kind of heat damage.

No used piston is perfect, but it should be free of deep scratches; wear should be confined to the thrust faces, which are the two areas 90 degrees from the wrist pin centerline. Uneven or skewed wear marks may indicate a bent crankshaft or connecting rod.

Moped piston shapes are more complicated than they appear. The piston must be able to expand under temperature without binding against the bore. When cold, the crown is a few hundredths of a millimeter smaller than the base of the skirt, and the diameter measured along the wrist pin centerline is less than the diameter at the thrust faces. In other words, the piston is an ovoid cone. Once the engine starts, the piston expands to make nearly full contact with the bore.

Where the piston is measured is up to the discretion of the manufacturer: half do not even give the piston-bore clearance, let

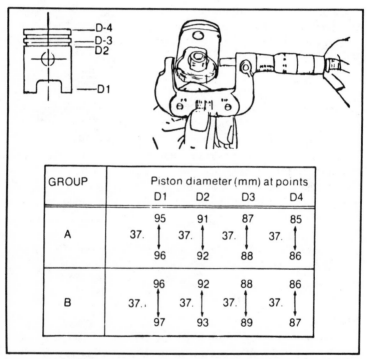

| GROUP | Piston diameter (mm) at points | | | |
	D1	D2	D3	D4
A	37. 95↕96	37. 91↕92	37. 87↕88	37. 85↕86
B	37.. 96↕97	37. 92↕93	37. 88↕89	37. 86↕87

Fig. 8-15. Measurement points and piston diameter specifications for the Tomas engine. Readings range from 37.97 mm (max.) for skirt diameter on a Group "B" piston to 37.85 mm (min.) for crown diameter on a Group "A".

alone how they arrive at it. Those that supply a clearance specification usually want the measurement taken at the base of the piston, across the thrust faces. In other words, the largest dimension is used as the guide. Tomas specifies four measuring points (Fig. 8-15).

Experience and the available data suggests that chromed bores tolerate much smaller clearances than plain cast iron. The typical chromed engine is set up at 0.015-0.035 mm (0.0006-0.0013 in.), while cast iron requires 0.060-0.070 mm (0.0024-0.0028 in.). The porous chrome used on these cylinders holds more oil than iron.

Remove the rings from the piston, noting which side is up. The top side should be stamped with an identifying letter near the gap. Handle rings with care, for the edges are razor sharp. Snap one of the rings and, holding it with a file handle or Vise-Grips, use it to clean the grooves. Do not remove metal.

Insert a new ring into each of the grooves and measure the flank clearance with a feeler gauge. It is easier to get an accurate measurement if the ring is backed into the groove as shown in Fig. 8-16. Flank clearance should be between 0.03-0.07 mm (0.001-0.003 in.) Much more than this can cause breakage from ring flutter.

Disassembly

Before removing the piston from the connecting rod, mark the leading edge of the crown for guidance in reassembly. Some pistons are already stamped with the letter S or F; most are not. The engine will run with a piston installed backwards, but after a few miles will knock.

The wrist pin is secured in the piston by two spring clips, known

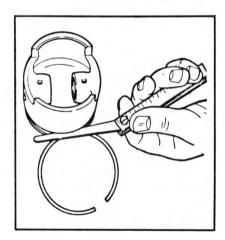

Fig. 8-16. Checking ring flank clearance. Courtesy Kohler of Kohler.

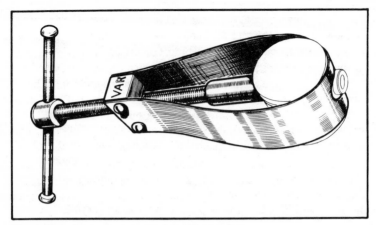

Fig. 8-17. A piston pin extractor from Motobecane.

in the trade as *circlips*. Place a rag in the block cavity and extract the circlips with long-nosed pliers. If you drop one, the rag will prevent it from falling into the engine. Discard the circlips: they are too important to be trusted twice.

There are several ways of removing the wrist pin. The easiest way is with a pin extractor, shown in Fig. 8-17. The tool is available from any moped importer and from Kohler engine dealers. Another method is to heat the piston with an electric hot plate or propane torch. If you use a torch, keep the flame moving in circles around the upper diameter of the piston. Stop when the piston smokes. Once heated, the piston will expand enough to release the wrist pin. Do not simply drive the pin out with a punch, for even if you take pains to support the back side of the connecting rod, some rod distortion is almost inevitable. Some manufacturers insist that the piston be cooled in the cylinder to prevent distortion.

The *rod eye*, or small-end, bearing takes several forms. It may be a bushing, a caged needle bearing, or merely a collection of needles. If your engine has free needles, be careful not to lose any as the pin is forced past the rod eye. Above all, do *not* allow any needles to drop into the block.

If you wish to replace the piston, you must use one in the same tolerance group. If the cylinder is worn, you be able to go to a larger diameter. Pistons and wrist pins are best purchased as a matched set. Most moped manufacturers supply wrist pins in two diameters; some supply three. Pins are identified by a color code or by letters stamped on the underside of one pin boss.

Oil the wrist pin and bearings. Position loose needles in the rod eye with grease or, better, beeswax. Warm the piston and slide the pin home. Use new circlips, compressing them just enough to clear the pin bores. Once the circlips are in place, turn them to see that they track in their grooves.

RINGS

Modern rings have a definite top and bottom, indicated by a code letter on the top side. Engines with chrome bores use unplated cast-iron rings; those with iron bores may use chrome rings. Do not interchange the two types. Unless indicated on the parts package, both rings are identical.

Insert each of the new rings about midway into the bore, using the back of the piston as a pilot to keep the ring square. Measure the gap between the ring ends—the specification varies with manufacturer and bore type (Fig. 8-18). Chromed engines are typically set up tight, with 0.30 mm (0.01 in.) gap. Cast-iron blocks go as wide as 0.80 mm (0.03 in.) Large gaps allow blowby into the crankcase, but some clearance is needed for ring growth under heat. The minimum dimension is 0.15 mm (0.006 in.). If the gap is excessive, suspect that the bore is worn; if it is too small and the ring ends almost touch, check that you have the correct parts. It may be necessary to file the ends, but don't get carried away.

Install the lower or No. 2 ring, slipping it over the top of the piston and past the No. 1 groove. Do not pull the ends farther apart than necessary to clear the piston diameter. Above all, do not twist

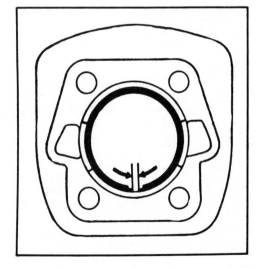

Fig. 8-18. The ring end gap is critical. Courtesy Batavus Bikeways Inc.

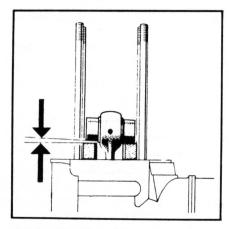

Fig. 8-19. Check rod trueness with the help of machinist's blocks and a new wrist pin. Courtesy Steyr-Daimler-Puch of America Corp.

the ring. Position the ends on each side of the locating pin and repeat the operation for the second ring.

CONNECTING ROD

The piston should pivot by its own weight on the small-end bearing. Steady the rod with one hand and, holding the piston with your thumb and forefinger over the wrist pin ends, move it up and down on the rod. There should be no more than a suggestion of vertical play between the small end bearing and the wrist pin. Holding the piston as before, try to wobble it in a vertical arc parallel to the wrist pin. More than a thirty-secondth of an inch movement means that the small-end bearing is bell-mouthed and should be replaced.

Needle bearings are not difficult to install; *bushings* are another matter. The new bushing is pressed into place, drilled for oil supply, and reamed for a pin clearance of 0.003 mm (0.0001 inch). Unless you have the tools, it is wise to have a dealer install the bushing.

The connecting rod swings on roller bearings at the crankpin. To get some idea of the condition of these bearings, bring the rod up to top dead center and move it up and down on the crankpin. Some play in the bearing is necessary, but you should not feel the rod release and stop. In other words, if the play is such that you can accelerate the rod with your hand, the bearing is shot. Try to move the connecting rod in an arc paralleling the crankpin. If the total arc is more than one-eighth inch, the big-end bearings have tapered and should be renewed.

Check rod straightness with a pair of machinist's blocks and a new wrist pin (Fig. 8-19). Compensate for possible crankcase distor-

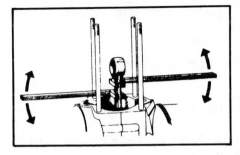

Fig. 8-20. Bend the rod as necessary. Courtesy Steyr-Daimler-Puch of America Corp.

tion by switching the blocks from one side of the rod to the other. The rod can be straightened with a homemade bending bar (Fig. 8-20).

LOWER END

The lower end includes the crankcase, crankshaft, main bearings seals, and the big end of the connecting rod. Lower end repairs are serious matters, not entered into lightly. Some special tools are needed.

PULLING THE ENGINE

Lower end work requires that the engine be taken out of the frame. The engine is secured by bolts and mated to the frame at the fuel, electrical, exhaust, and drive systems. Disconnect these parts:

- Fuel line
- Throttle cable
- Choke cable (if fitted)
- Compression release cable (if fitted)
- Alternator—usually a single, multiprong connection aft of the flywheel
- Exhaust pipe
- Chain or belt

The belt spring complicates matters on Peugeot bikes. The spring must be compressed by tilting the engine to the rear and then slowly released. Once the fairings, a carburetor, compression release cable, and wiring are dismantled, follow this procedure:

- Insert special tool No. 69260 into the flywheel hub and one of the sprocket teeth (Fig. 8-21).

- Push down on the right-hand pedal crank to tip the engine toward the rear of the vehicle.
- Carefully remove the belt.
- Raise the pedal and tip the engine toward the front wheel, releasing tension on the spring.
- Remove the tool.
- Carefully undo the support plate fixing bolts, completely disarming the spring.
- Push out the engine holddown bolt with a 9.5 mm diameter rod, which locks the support arm in place.
- Now pull the rod back far enough to release the engine. Once the engine is free, insert the rod its full length through the control arm.

Drain the transmission and snug down the drain plug (more than one engine has been ruined by a drain plug that was run in finger-tight and forgotten). Clean oil and road grime from the engine castings. These and subsequent operations go faster if the engine is mounted in a holding fixture. Figure 8-22 shows a simple, easy-to-fabricate stand and a top-of-the-line, fully adjustable model.

CRANKCASE

Moped engines are traditionally split vertically through a parting line that divides the crankcases into left- and right-hand pairs. Puch and Sachs engines are built on the more modern horizontal pattern, with the parting line passing through the main bearings. With the exception of Velosolex (discussed in a separate section

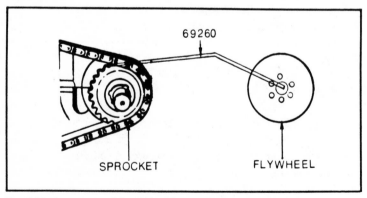

Fig. 8-21. Peugeot special tool No. 69260 is a convenience when removing the engine.

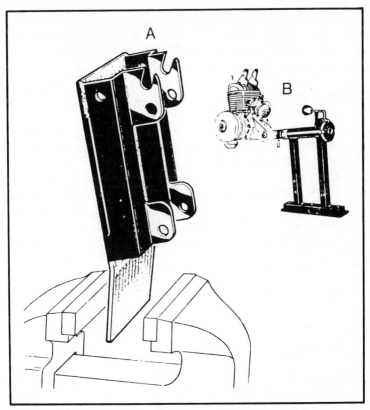

Fig. 8-22. Engine stands range from the spartan Velosolex model (view A) to the elaborate Peugeot stand which allows the engine to be rotated (view B).

below) vertically split engines are difficult to open because rotating components—flywheel, sprocket, clutch drum, and the like—must be removed from at least one end of the shafts, and main and transmission bearings are pressed into the crankcase halves.

Vertical Pattern

Unless the engine is to be completely stripped, work from the flywheel side. The operations involve disassembly of the stator plate (Fig. 8-23). Mark the stator and the crankcase so that proper timing will be retained when the engine is reassembled.

Clutch and Pedal Assembly. Remove at least one pedal arm assembly, tapping out the pinch bolt with a brass punch, and file any burrs that may be left on the pedal shaft. Burrs could damage the oil seal. If required, remove the sprocket and the clutch assembly.

Most sprockets are held by bolts and splines; a few have the additional security of a taper fit. Figure 8-24 shows a sprocket extractor. Clutches are (almost universally) pressed on tapered shafts; a few are held by splines and snap (Seegar) rings. Pressed clutches are withdrawn with a smaller version of the familiar flywheel extractor. These tools are sometimes available from bicycle dealers as well as moped distributors.

Crankcase Disassembly. The cases are held together by four lines of defense—through-bolts, alignment pins, gasket binds, and the press-fit of the main bearings. Through-bolts are no particular problem: once the nuts are loosened, the bolts can be tapped out with a soft drift. Nor should the pins be of much concern; however, if the pin holes are open on both sides, the pins can be driven out, releasing some tension on the case halves. The gasket will just have to be broken. The press-fit of the main bearings is a major difficul-

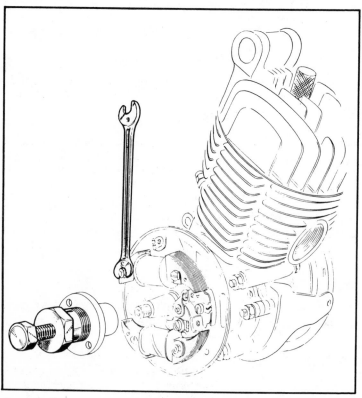

Fig. 8-23. Removing a Motobecane stator plate. The plate and block should be indexed to ensure correct timing upon assembly.

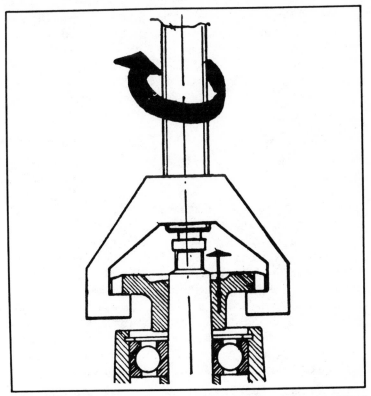

Fig. 8-24. An extractor is needed for the few engines that have taper-fitted sprockets.

ty that has to be overcome without damage to the shafts or case. There are three ways to do this:

The bearing fit on some engines is loose enough that the cases can be jarred apart with a soft mallet. A few glancing blows around the edges of the castings softens things up; the job is finished by driving the crankshaft stub out. Figure 8-25 shows the operation on a Garelli engine.

A variation on this technique is to heat the casting adjacent to the bearing with a propane torch (Fig. 8-26). The illustration shows a Motorbecane crankcase half with a single bearing. If you are dealing with a case that supports a transmission bearing as well, it too must be heated. Keep the torch circling around the bearing bosses and stop when the case begins to smoke. Too much heat will fatally distort it. Once the case has expanded, relaxing its grip on the bearings, drive the shafts out with a mallet.

The third alternative is to press the crankshaft out with a threaded tool that bolts to the engine casting. Figure 8-27 illustrates three such tools. The first drawing shows an extractor for Peugeot engines; the second, a similar tool sized for the Minarelli V1; the third drawing illustrates a nearly universal model from Bolger Manufacturing. Intended to service Honda 125/250-cc. motorcycles, the Bolger tool can be drilled to fit most moped engines. It is available from cycle dealers.

Bearings. The bearings remain on their shafts, which are anchored to a case half. Look very carefully at the bearing bosses on the loose case half. *Axial scores,* scores running the same direction as the centerlines of the shafts—are caused by forcing the bearings out of the case. Unless the aluminum is plowed and raised, axial scores have no significance. If high spots are present, smooth them with a fine half-round file to make assembly easier.

Radial scores, running around the inner diameter of the bosses, mean trouble. The bearing races have broken the interference fit on their bosses, either because the bearings have failed or because the boss diameter and the outer diameter of the races was not controlled properly during manufacture. Disassemble the other side of the engine to check the bosses there. If the bosses are badly spun, look around for another engine. Slight wear, on the order of 0.010 inch, can be corrected by coating the outside diameter of the bear-

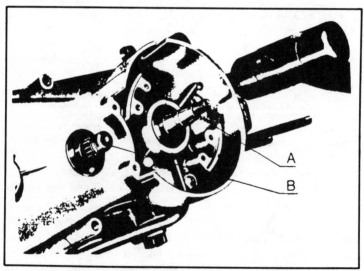

Fig. 8-25. Garelli engines can be opened with a soft-faced mallet applied to the crankshaft (A) and output shaft (B) ends.

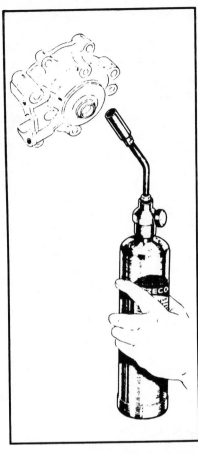

Fig. 8-26. Heating a Motobecane crankcase. It is assumed that the seal will be replaced.

ing races with Loctite Stud n' Seal just before assembly. Once the parts are bolted down and air is excluded, Loctite hardens and holds the bearings fast. Do not get any Loctite on the rollers and balls.

Seals. New seals must be installed each time the cases are opened. Pry out the old ones with a screwdriver, being careful not to scratch the seal bosses. Seals are installed with the cupped side out, away from crankcase pressure. Factory code numbers are on the side from which the seal is driven. Seal drivers exist and should be used whenever possible. Figure 8-28 shows a collection of Peugeot drivers and pilots for the right- and left-hand cases. A more typical driver is shown in Fig. 8-29.

Although factory tools make the work easier and help prevent the embarrassment of leaking seals on a newly overhauled engine, they are not absolutely essential. If the truth were known, probably most rebuilt moped engines have had their seals installed with a wooden dowel.

The seal must go home flat and to the same depth as the original. Some mechanics coat the seal boss with gasket cement. Once the seal is installed, the excess cement must be wiped off and the seal lips lubricated with clean motor oil or transmission fluid.

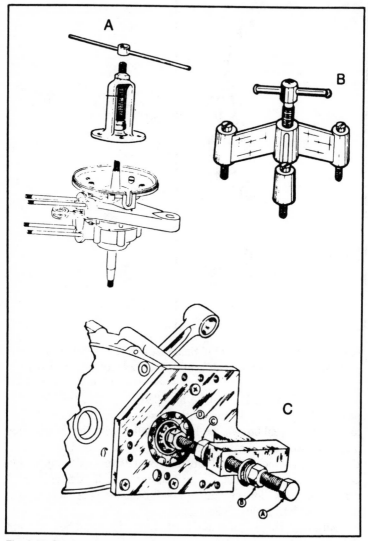

Fig. 8-27. Crankshaft extractor tools from Peugeot (view A), Minarelli (view B), and Bolger Manufacturing (view C).

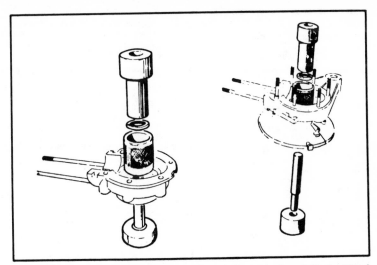

Fig. 8-28. Peugeot tools make seal installation almost foolproof. Each side of the engine is dimensioned differently and requires its own anvils, pilots, and drivers.

Protect the lips by covering crankshaft keyways, splines, and other sharp irregularities with a layer of masking tape.

Gasket. Mount a new gasket on one crankcase half; the gasket should be soaked in oil first. Heat the bearing bosses on the

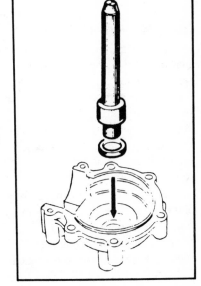

Fig. 8-29. Most seal drivers are simple one-piece tools like this one from Motobecane.

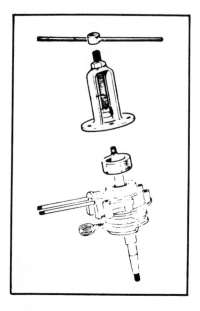

Fig. 8-30. Assembling the crank-cases is easier if the crankshaft is pulled into place.

outboard case, using a large washer to shield the new seal from flame. If one is available, use an extractor tool to pull the crankshaft and inner case into the outer case. Figure 8-30 illustrates the Peugeot setup for this operation. The end of the tool is threaded over the crankshaft and the spacer distributes stress over the circumference of the bearing boss.

Velosolex Vertical Pattern

Velosolex crankcases are split vertically, but other structural features of this engine put it in a class by itself. Once the cylinder barrel, fuel tank, fuel line, muffler, and carburetor are dismantled, opening the engine is merely a matter of removing the cover plate over the crankcase (Fig. 8-31). The plate is secured by eight capscrews and gasketed. It does not support the crankshaft, which rides on a single large bearing just inboard of the flywheel. Assemble with a new gasket and, working diagonally, torque the capscrews to 0.75 kgm (5.4 ft-lb).

In the event that you need to disassemble the power-takeoff side of the engine, fix the crankshaft with a stroke limiter, available from Velosolex as part No. 01213. Remove the drive roller, clutch, and oil seal. (These operations are described in detail in the next chapter.) Index the stator plate and crankcase to hold the timing dimension. Using Velosolex tool No. 00195, withdraw the stator plate, twisting

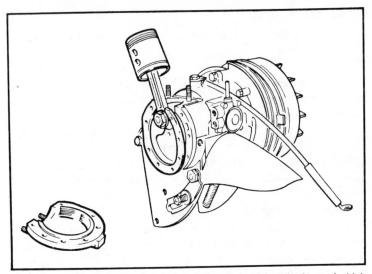

Fig. 8-31. Velosolex engines are unique in many ways, not the least of which is the absence of a second main bearing.

it as shown in Fig. 8-32. Heat the crankcase at the bearing boss with a propane torch. When the case begins to smoke, it is warm enough, and the crankshaft can be driven out with a few mallet blows.

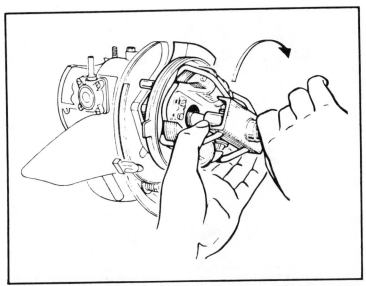

Fig. 8-32. The Velosolex stator plate is removed with special tool No. 01213.

167

Horizontal Pattern

Puch and Sachs engines have horizontally split crankcases that can be opened as easily as a can of sardines. Drain the transmission lubricant, remove the cylinder barrel and external engine covers, and undo the holddown screws or bolts. The upper crankcase casting lifts off. Crankshaft, bearings, seals, connecting rod, and piston come out as an assembly.

Clean the crankcases in solvent and carefully inspect the bearing bosses for evidence that the bearings have spun. Loctite Stud n' Seal will compensate for some bearing wear and, as long as the bearings themselves are serviceable, will prevent reoccurrence of the problem.

The Sachs engine is set up to eliminate end loads on the bearings (Fig. 8-33). Clearance between the bearings and the flywheels is zero, or should be. There are three dimensions involved: distance between the outer edges of the bearings (57.75 mm (2.273 in.)); distance between the outer edges of the flywheels (34.20 mm (1.346 in.)); and combined width of the bearings (22.00 mm (0.866 in.)). Adding the distance between the flywheels and the width of the bearings determines how thick the shims should be. In the case above, the bearings and flywheels account for 56.20 mm (2.212 in.)—1.55 mm (0.061 in.) shy of the 57.75-mm requirement. The shortfall must be supplied by shims. Place the shims between the

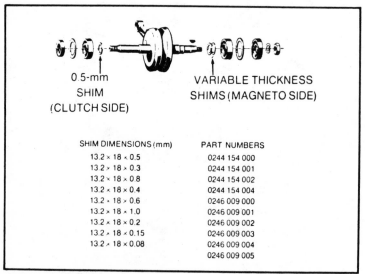

0.5-mm SHIM (CLUTCH SIDE)

VARIABLE THICKNESS SHIMS (MAGNETO SIDE)

SHIM DIMENSIONS (mm)	PART NUMBERS
13.2 × 18 × 0.5	0244 154 000
13.2 × 18 × 0.3	0244 154 001
13.2 × 18 × 0.8	0244 154 002
13.2 × 18 × 0.4	0244 154 004
13.2 × 18 × 0.6	0246 009 000
13.2 × 18 × 1.0	0246 009 001
13.2 × 18 × 0.2	0246 009 002
13.2 × 18 × 0.15	0246 009 003
13.2 × 18 × 0.08	0246 009 004
	0246 009 005

Fig. 8-33. The shim arrangement for the Sachs 501/1 series engine.

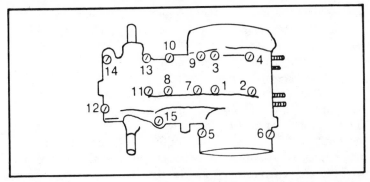

Fig. 8-34. Sachs has developed this torque sequence to prevent crankcase distortion.

bearings and the flywheels, with the 0.5 mm (0.020 in.) shim on the clutch side and any others needed on the magneto side. Once the crankshaft is shimmed, it can be installed in the lower case. Snug up all the fasteners and, following the sequence in Fig. 8-34, torque to 1.0-1.2 kgm (7.2-8.7 ft-lb).

Puch engines are assembled without reference to thrust washers (other than to be sure that any that are present remain). The only variable is the position of the magneto-side crankshaft seal. It must be approximately a quarter inch outboard of the main bearing; otherwise the bearing will starve for oil (Fig. 8-35).

MAIN BEARINGS

Anti-friction (ball and roller) bearings are manufactured with a clearance of approximately 0.0005 in. between the races and roll-

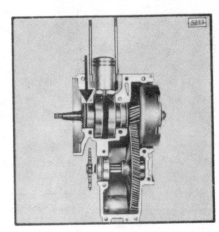

Fig. 8-35. Leave a generous clearance between the main bearing and flywheel-side seal on the Puch engine.

ing elements. Unfortunately, changes in clearance cannot be measured directly, and the mechanic must rely on intuition and experience.

The bearings must be clean and dry for assembly. Use a good grade of solvent—trichlorethylene, if you have it—and allow the bearings to air-dry: rags or paper towels dirty the bearings with lint and dust. Drying can be speeded with filtered compressed air; the air line should have at least one recently serviced water trap between the nozzle and the compressor. Play the air stream over the bearings, but not against the races. Bearings spinning under a jet of high pressure air generate interesting gyroscopic effects, but almost always are damaged in the process.

Using a wooden dowel, try to pry the outer race off the balls. If the race comes free easily, you can be sure the bearing is worn

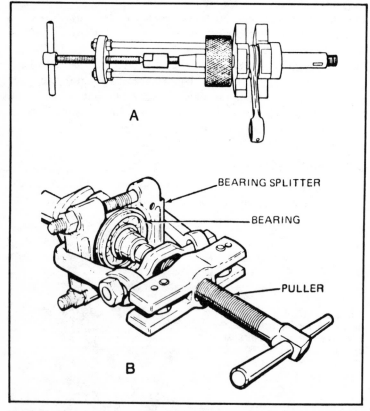

Fig. 8-36. A bearing puller supplied by Batavus (view A) and the more readily available bearing splitter (view B).

out of tolerance. Slowly turn the outer races. If the action is rough or catchy, replace the bearing.

Main bearings do not wear at the same rate. The power take-off bearing takes the worst beating and, unless there is a problem, such as a bent crankshaft or off-balance flywheel, should fail first. It is only reasonable to replace main bearings as a set.

Figure 8-36 shows a Batavus-supplied bearing puller. It is typical of moped tools in that the jaws are very thin to reach behind bearings that are cheek-to-jowl with the flywheels. Tools of this type must be ordered from the importer. The bearing splitter in view B is an auto mechanic's tool that can be adapted to all but the most crowded moped engines. Bearing splitters are available from auto supply houses and from most franchised rental agencies.

In any event, do not give in to impatience and try to wedge the bearings loose. You may get them off this way, but the crankshaft will suffer in the process.

Heat the replacement bearings in a container of oil, keeping the temperature well under the boiling point. The bearings should be supported on a wire mesh, so that they do not come into contact with the sides and bottom of the container. For reasons of safety, the operation should be carried on outdoors. Install the warm bearings with the help of a *driver* (Fig. 8-37). You can use a factory tool or a clean length of pipe whose diameter matches the inner race. Do not apply force to the balls or outer race. The side of the bearing that has been reinforced to withstand the rigors of installation carries an identification number and the manufacturer's logo. The inboard side is blank and, depending upon the machine, may have a distinctive profile (Fig. 8-38).

CRANKSHAFT

Mopeds use built-up crankshafts with the crankpin pressed into the flywheels. This means that the connecting rod is stronger than it would otherwise be and that there is potential for crankshaft misalignment. It also means that replacing the crankpin (big-end) bearings is a formidable operation on machines other than the Velosolex.

Alignment

Serious misalignment can be detected with the crankshaft installed. Mount a dial indicator on the casting as shown in Fig. 8-39 and watch the needle deflection as the crank is turned. A total deflec-

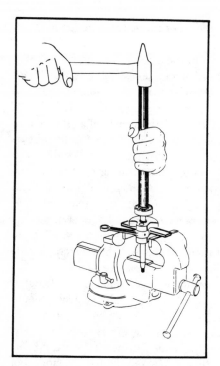

Fig. 8-37. Installing a main bearing on a Motobecane crankshaft. Note that the driver rides against the inner race.

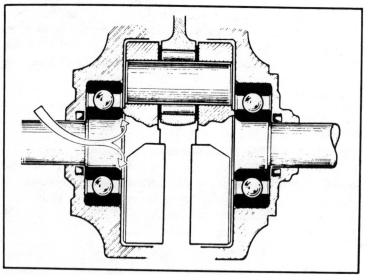

Fig. 8-38. Bearings have a definite up and down side as indicated by the manufacturer's name and bearing identification code. Motobecane is restrictively definite and has arranged matters so the bearings will seize if installed wrong.

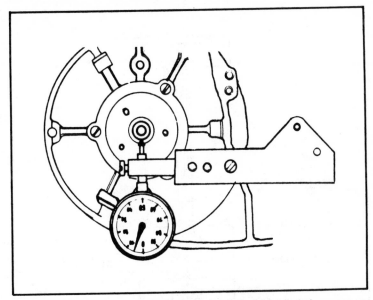

Fig. 8-39. Dial indicator readings with the crankshaft installed give some notion of crankshaft alignment, although the results are compromised by main bearing wear.

tion of more than 0.002 inch should be corrected. Repeat the operation on the other end of the crankshaft.

A more accurate method, and one that *must* be used if the crank is to be straightened, involves two precision V-blocks and a pair of dial indicators. The position of the dial indicators, the distance of the V-blocks from the flywheels, and the distance between the wheels are critical dimensions, although the last one is sacrificed for shaft alignment (Fig. 8-40). In other words, some wheel wobble is tolerated to make the shafts run true.

The wheels are pried away from each other with wooden wedges, and the distance between them closed with a C-clamp or with judicious blows from a brass hammer. Figure 8-41 shows the relationship between indicator readings and wheel spacing.

CONNECTING ROD BEARING

Play in the big-end bearing can be detected once the cylinder barrel is off. (See "Cylinder Barrels" for details.) As a further check, spin the rod completely around the crankpin. Roughness or rattle means that the bearings and possibly the crankpin and connecting rod must be replaced.

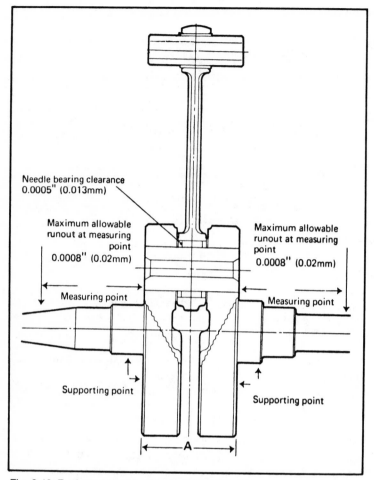

Fig. 8-40. For best accuracy, the crankshaft should be cradled on precision-ground V-blocks, spaced equidistantly from the flywheels. Dial indicators mounted near the ends of the stub shafts completes the set-up.

Velosolex

Install the stroke limiter (or an equivalent metric bolt) in the side of the crankcase as shown in Fig. 8-42. Mark the outboard side of the piston as an assembly aid. Remove the 14-mm nut and washer. Lift the piston off the crankpin and extract the bushing. Install a new bushing—flat side toward the crank web—and flood the assembly with oil. Install the connecting rod, washer, and nut. In severely worn engines, the washer and connecting rod should also be replaced. Torque the nut to 1.70 kgm (12.3 ft-lb).

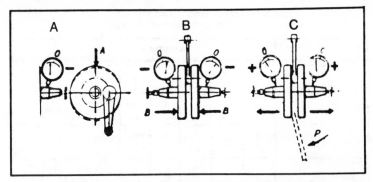

Fig. 8-41. Possible misalignments and their cures: If one stub shaft is high, drive its flywheel down with a brass hammer (view A); If both shafts are low, squeeze the wheels together (view B); if both shafts are high, pry the wheels apart. Note that the crankpin is the fulcrum around which the adjustments are made.

Other Engines

Any moped crankshaft can be disassembled with the help of a 10-ton arbor press, but most manufacturers do not trust service personnel with this exacting work. The factory provides exchange crankshaft assemblies (Batavus) or simply sells the customer a new

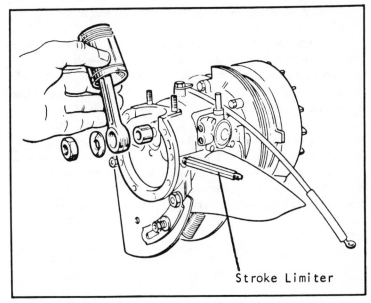

Fig. 8-42. Velosolex connecting rods are secured by a single 14mm nut and thrust washer.

Table 8-5. Jawa Babetta Connecting Rod,
Crankpin Bearing, and Crankpin Compatibility.

Connecting rod	Assembly groups						
I	10 A	9 B	8 C	7 D	6 E	Roller	Pin
II	9 A	8 B	7 C	6 D	5 E	Roller	Pin
III	8 A	7 B	6 C	5 D	4 E	Roller	Pin
IV	7 A	6 B	5 C	4 D	3 E	Roller	Pin
V	6.7 A	5.6 B	4.5 C	3.4 D	2.3 E	Roller	Pin

crankshaft assembly, already aligned and ready to be installed. Other manufacturers will provide crankpins, big-end bearing sets, and connecting rods, but complications arise when parts are installed separately and not as matched sets.

Table 8-5 illustrates the choices available for the Babetta engine. There are five connecting rods, graded by the diameter of the big-end bearing surface, five crankpins, and 13 roller bearing diameters. If you have a grade I con rod, a grade 6 roller set, and a grade D pin, the clearance will be wrong. With that rod and roller set only a grade E pin works.

The factories are a long way from American shores, and it is always wise to obtain the parts before the crankshaft is dismantled. Note the depth of the pin in the face of the flywheels; on most, the pin is flush and never stands proud of the wheels. Mount the crankshaft in a fixture, supporting the inside cheek of the uppermost wheel. Mark the wheels with a straight edge and chalk as an assembly guide. Press the pin out of one wheel and then out of the remaining one. Press a new pin in place, mount the bearing and connecting rod. Press work is finished when the remaining wheel is installed. Align the crankshaft as described above and flood the new bearing with oil before installing the crankshaft in the engine.

Chapter 9

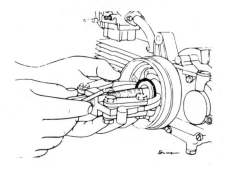

Drive Line

Power is transmitted in strange and devious ways in a moped. There are two power sources—human and mechanical. Human power is used to start the engine, help it when it falters, and, if necessary, can become the sole means of propulsion. The engine is the primary power source, connected to the rear wheel by means of an automatic clutch. In addition, some mopeds have automatic torque-multiplying transmissions, so the engine can operate at its most efficient rpm regardless of the forward speed of the vehicle.

CENTRIFUGAL CLUTCHES

The basic clutch mechanism is *centrifugal*, engaging in response to engine or pedal crank speed. The details vary enormously between makes, but all have these features in common:

- A central hub or yoke that turns at engine speed.
- A drum, which is connected to the load.
- Friction shoes or plates that connect the hub with the drum.
- An override mechanism to transfer power from rider to the engine to start it. The override may be at the clutch or at some remote spot on the drive line.

Now we'll take a look at several popular clutches.

Batavus M 48

The M 48 clutch has been influential in moped technology; one manufacturer has gone so far as to produce an almost identical copy.

Operation. The clutch hub, spring, pressure plate, and end plate turn with the crankshaft (Fig. 9-1). The "house," or drum and clutch plate, are connected to the rear wheel by a belt and chain. At low engine speeds, the drum floats on the crankshaft, insulated from motion by the needle bearing. As speed increases, ball bearings packed into the clutch spring feel the tug of centrifugal force and move outward, stretching the spring in the process. Ramps on the outer edge of the clutch hub divert this outward motion; the balls push to the left against the pressure plate. While the plate turns at engine speed with the hub, its splines allow some axial movement, and the plate contacts the right-hand friction surface on the clutch plate. The drum begins to receive power. Continued motion of the balls forces the clutch plate to the right, where it contacts the end plate. Because the end plate is bolted to the crankshaft, no further axial movement is possible; the clutch plate is sandwiched between the pressure and end plates. Full torque goes to the drum and, hence, to the back wheel.

The starting lever displaces the end, clutch, and pressure plates to the right. Once the pressure plate butts against the spring and ball assembly, no further axial movement is possible: the clutch plate is trapped between the two hub-mounted plates. Power enters at the hub, passes through the clutch plate, and then to the crankshaft.

Service. The only internal adjustment is the clearance between the override lever and the thrust button. Bend the lever to obtain 2.0 mm (0.80 in.) clearance in the disengaged position (Fig. 9-2).

Upon disassembly, clean the parts in solvent—except the clutch disc, which should not be wetted. Clutch slippage problems can usually be corrected by replacing the disc. Refusal to disengage completely or harsh, abrupt engagement most often involves the end and side plates. Replace if the plates are warped, scored, or streaked with blue temper marks. Small imperfections can be polished out with crocus cloth. Check the needle bearing for excessive play and, if necessary, replace with a new bearing, driven in from the marked side. Fill the bearing with high temperature grease or heavy transmission oil. Oil the hub, ball and spring assembly, and bronze thrust piece, but do not get any oil on the disc or the pressure sides of the plates.

Note: Use the seal protector shown in Fig. 9-3 when mounting

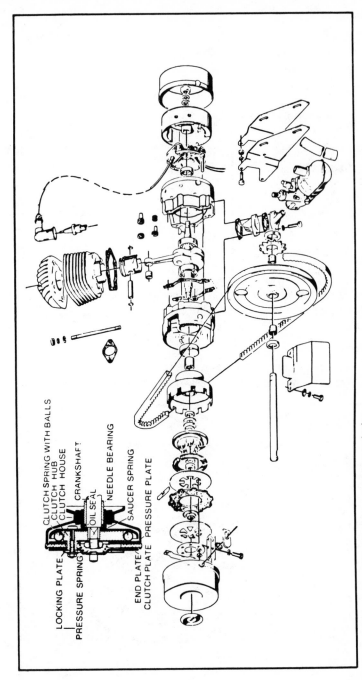

CLUTCH SPRING WITH BALLS
CLUTCH HUB
CLUTCH HOUSE
CRANKSHAFT
OIL SEAL
NEEDLE BEARING
SAUCER SPRING
LOCKING PLATE
PRESSURE SPRING
END PLATE
CLUTCH PLATE PRESSURE PLATE

Fig. 9-1. The Batavus M 48 engine and transmission.

179

Fig. 9-2. The override lever should be within 0.80 in. of the thrust button in the disengaged position. Bend the lever as required.

the hub. Otherwise, the seal may be damaged, a condition that leads to bearing failure from loss of lubricant.

Jawa

The Jawa clutch employs shoes rather than a friction disc.

Operation. There are two sets of shoes: the outboard assembly

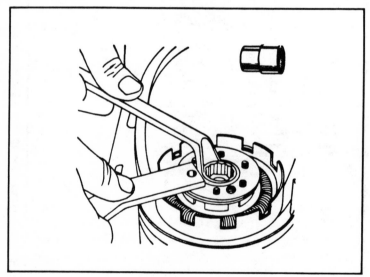

Fig. 9-3. The M 48 clutch wrench and seal protector.

connects the engine with the drive train; the inboard set transfers power from the pedals, via the drive chain. Figure 9-4 shows the arrangement of parts. The flywheel (1), drive clutch shoes (3), segment carrier (4), and sleeve (5) are fixed to the crankshaft and turn with it. The starting shoes (6) and the clutch drum (7) are geared to the drive system and can turn independently of the crankshaft.

During starting, power enters the clutch drum, spinning it and the starting shoes, which are pivoted on the drum. At approximately 600 rpm, the starting shoes engage the inner lip of the segment carrier, turning it and the flywheel. Once the engine catches, power enters through the segment carrier. The drive clutch shoes pivot out against the garter spring and meet the clutch drum.

Service. Remove the flywheel bolt and the three clutch holddown bolts (Fig. 9-5A). Lift the flywheel off and, using special tool No. 975 1000 1.2, withdraw the segment carrier (Fig. 9-5B). (A substitute for this tool is a steel plate drilled for the segment carrier bolts with a large nut welded over the center). Remove the sleeve with a small gear puller (Fig. 9-5C); if the shoes are to be separated, assemble them on their springs before installation. Pick out the oil seal and withdraw the drum (Fig. 9-5E).

Although some oil seeps past the seal, it should not get on the friction surfaces. If the seal should fail, the clutch will drip oil.

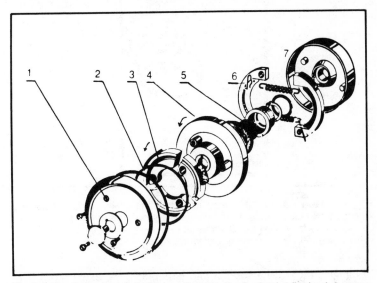

Fig. 9-4. The Jawa clutch is tucked neatly under the flywheel. 1-flywheel; 2-garter (shoe-return) spring; 3-drive clutch shoes; 4-segment carrier; 5-sleeve; 6-starting shoes; 7-clutch drum.

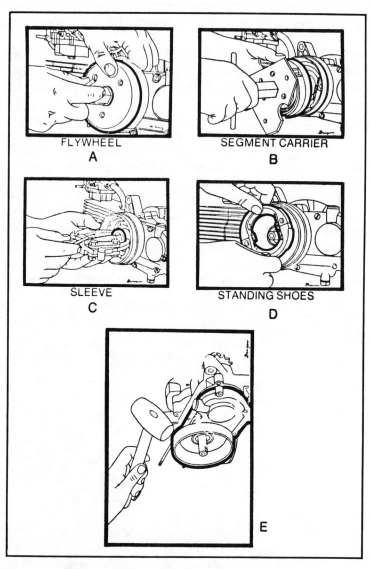

Fig. 9-5. Jawa clutch service sequence. Undo the three holddown bolts and the central nut (view A); withdraw the segment carrier with the factory tool or a reasonable facsimile (view B); extract the sleeve (view C); lift out the starting shoes (view D); remove the oil seal (view E).

Engagement will be sudden and harsh, and the drive shoes may smoke under load. The seal and both sets of shoes should be replaced; in a pinch you can replace the seal and dry the linings with repeated applications of Berkebile 2 + 2 Gum Cutter.

Unless there is an oil problem, the starting shoes can be ignored: they get little wear. The drive shoes should be replaced long before the lining has worn down to metal, because once this happens, the drum will be ruined. Early signs of wear are late engagement and clutch slip on hills.

A stretched garter spring allows the drive shoes to engage early, before the engine is up to speed. Replace the spring and examine the shoes and drum for signs of overheating.

Peugeot

The Peugeot clutch is uniquely Peugeot, with features that are shared by none other, yet it is very practical device, having proved itself over millions of miles.

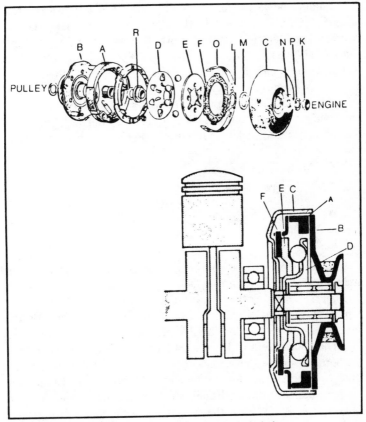

Fig. 9-6. Peugeot clutch in cross-section and exploded views.

183

Operation. Figure 9-6 illustrates the mechanism in cutaway and exploded views. It must be remembered that the clutch drum C, and ball drum D bolt to the crankshaft and turn with it. Starting shoes A and clutch disc F turn with the drive pulley B.

During starting, power flows from the pedals to the drive pulley. At about 5 mph, the starting shoes A cam out against the drum C, locking the pulley and crankshaft. Once the engine starts, the six ball bearings move out toward the edge of the spinning ball drum D. The bearings are confined to teardrop shaped holes; as they move outward, they cam out of the holes and press against the plate E. The plate moves the clutch disc F against a lip on the inner edge of the drum. Power flows from the drum, to the disc, and through splines on the rim of the disc to the drive pulley. The star spring keeps the plate away from the disc at low rpm.

Service. The clutch mechanism is essentially the same for single and variable-ratio machines. Hold the clutch drum with a strap wrench (Fig. 9-7) and remove the 17-mm nut (right-hand thread: overhand and left to loosen). Remove the washers and replace the nut with special tool No. 69142. This tool keeps things together when the pulley is removed and takes the guess work out of clutch adjustments. Remove the pulley.

Holding the ball drum D and plate E with one hand, unthread the special tool and pull the clutch drum off. Mark the outboard side of the clutch disc if it is to be reused. Remove parts in this order:

- Disc F
- Spring L
- Adjusting washer M
- Drum C
- Washer N

Place the pulley assembly on a bench, pulley down. Remove the nuts holding the locking ring O and lockwashers, and remove the locking ring. Unhook the springs from the studs in the shoes, noting which of the two studs was used (the first is for direct-drive machines; the second for variable-ratio models).

The shoes are a little tricky. Lightly lubricate the shoe pivot anchors. Assemble the springs on the shoes, with the large hooked ends secured by the slots in the shoes. Mount the shoes on their anchors and hook the small ends of the springs over the appropriate pins. Correctly installed, the open sides of the hooks face toward the center of pulley plate B. Secure the shoes to the plate with two

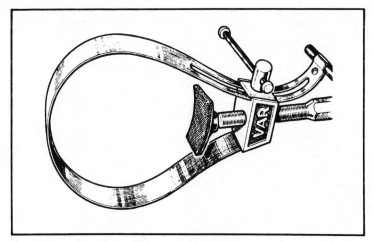

Fig. 9-7. A flywheel holder supplied by Motobecane.

5-mm nuts and lockwashers. The nuts must be turned so their sides are clear of the clutch disc.

Assemble the rest of the mechanism, reversing the disassembly sequence. Torque the outboard nut 4.0 ts kgm (28.9 ft-lb) and test. If the clutch behaves abnormally—engaging harshly or slipping under load—it will be necessary to check the clearance between pressure plate E and disc F. There are at least three ways to do this.

The clutch can be partially assembled with the help of special tools Nos. 69140 and 69141. This is the currently accepted shop practice.

The clutch can be assembled in reverse of normal order on the crankshaft. One special tool, formerly available as No. 42018, is needed. This tool can be fabricated from a discarded clutch drum.

Assemble the clutch with modeling clay between the pressure plate and the clutch lining. Disassemble and measure the thickness of the clay.

The specification is 0.5-0.7 mm (0.020-0.028 in.). Correct by substituting a different-thickness adjusting washer. (Table 9-1).

If you use method 1, place the assembling shaft 69141 vertically in a vise and assemble these parts on it:

- Washer N
- Adjusting plate No. 69140
- Adjusting washer M
- Spring L
- Disc F

Table 9-1. Clutch Washer Specs.

Thickness	Washer Part Number
0.40 mm	45818
0.60 mm	45819
0.80 mm	45820
1.00 mm	45821

- Pressure plate E
- Balls
- Ball drum D
- Nut

If you choose method 2, turn the engine on its side and assemble the parts in this inverted order:

- Hub ring R
- Ball drum D
- Balls
- Pressure plate E
- Clutch plate F
- Spring L
- Adjusting washer M
- Special tool No. 42018
- Washer N
- Washer P
- Nut K

Method 3 is, as you would expect, the most laborious. The clutch must be disassembled, assembled with modeling clay between disc F and the inboard side of drum C, disassembled again to remove the clay, and assembled one more time.

TRANSMISSIONS

One of the characteristics of mopeds is the high reduction ratio between the engine and the back wheel. The engine may scream at 5000 rpm-plus, but the road speed of the vehicle must be kept under 30 mph. The reduction is accomplished by gears or a pulley-and-belt arrangement. Some machines combine a belt with gears. Most transmissions give a single ratio between the engine and the driving wheel; a few have variable speeds, selected automatically in response to engine rpm.

Belt Drives

The traditional moped (French model) uses a V-belt to transmit engine power to the drive sprocket. Although this system may look primitive, it has some real advantages. Belt drive is silent, vibration-free, and tends to isolate the crankshaft and main bearings from drive shocks.

Service. The belt must be replaced at intervals. It is a good idea to carry a second belt, wrapped in aluminum foil, on the machine. The aluminum foil will keep the belt dry and free of oil, and will help to protect if from ozone attack.

V-belts transmit power by wedging their angled sides against the edges of the pulley grooves. In time, the belt wears and sinks deeper into the grooves, changing the ratio slightly. A machine with a worn belt will have a marginally higher speed than one that has just been fitted with a new belt; conversely, the bike with the new belt should have slightly better acceleration. Wear becomes serious when it is localized; when the blanks of the belt show dips and depressions, or when wear has progressed until the belt rides on the base of the pulley groove. Should this happen, the belt becomes a flat belt, with very little capacity to transmit power.

Belt dressing is one of those "shade-tree fixes" that help in the short run and cause additional problems down the road. This product, available from auto supply houses in aerosol cans, contains a powerful solvent that makes the belt stickier and better able to transmit power. In the process, the belt is softened and wears more rapidly, but it works and will get you home.

Pulley grooves also wear and contribute to the early demise of the belt. The groove flanks should be flat and narrow enough so that the belt is supported well above the base of the groove. Wear is more pronounced on the engine pulley, which is the smaller of the two.

Adjustment. Too much belt tension defeats the wedging action of the belt and loads the crankshaft and pulley bearings; too little tension allows the belt to hump and slip. Some machines do not have provision for belt adjustment, either because of the maker's confidence in steel-cored belts or because adjustment is maintained automatically by means of a spring. Peugeot and Motobecane are examples of the latter method: the engines are pivoted against springs.

In any event, the belt should have approximately one-quarter inch play under light thumb pressure (Fig. 9-8). The engine is the movable element; the large pulley remains fixed to the frame. Fig-

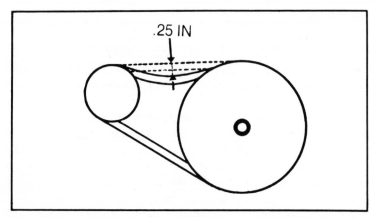

Fig. 9-8. Correct belt tension is important. Courtesy Batavus Bikeways, Inc.

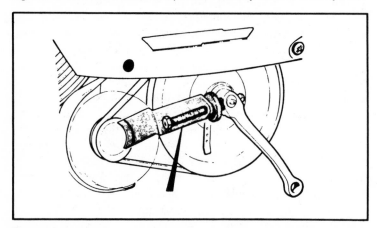

Fig. 9-9. A tool like this is convenient when adjusting belts against spring tension.

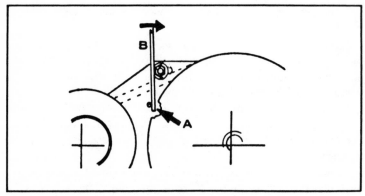

Fig. 9-10. Batavus belts are adjusted with the help of rod A and lever B.

ure 9-9 shows a very elegant tool used to pivot the engine away from the large pulley. The next drawing (Fig. 9-10) illustrates the Batavus procedure. Once the engine holddown bolts are slacked off, a 5-mm rod is inserted into hole A. Lever B rests against this rod and, moved as shown, pivots the engine forward.

Belt-Driven Variable-Speed Transmission

A belt running on fixed pulleys has some built-in ability to multiply torque. Figure 9-11 shows two pulleys with identical diameters. Under load, the lower side of the belt tenses and the upper side relaxes. The belt burrows more deeply into the driven pulley and flings outward on the drive pulley. The effective diameters of the pulleys change: the drive pulley becomes larger and the driven pulley shrinks. *Torque*, or turning force, is multiplied.

Although this feature is useful and gives a tractability to belt-driven machines that is absent with gear or friction drives, real torque multiplication requires some mechanical means of changing pulley diameter. Variable-speed transmissions, sometimes called *variators*, are used on snowmobiles, a few motorcycles, and on at least two light automobiles. These transmissions offer a fairly wide range of ratios and are entirely *stepless*. That is, one ratio blends into another without plateaus or steps.

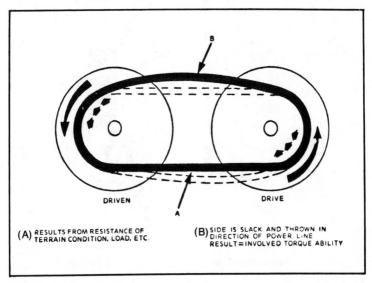

Fig. 9-11. Fixed pulleys benefit from some self-induced torque multiplication. Courtesy Bombardier Ltd.

Figure 9-12 illustrates an example from Peugeot. The inboard pulley flange (A) is fixed; the outboard flange (B) moves in and out. At low engine speeds, belt C rides low in the pulley groove, giving a low ratio for starting. As engine rpm increases, centrifugal force pivots the flyweights D out radially, camming the outboard flange inward. The belt is spring-loaded, and thus can respond by climbing higher in the groove. As it does, the ratio is raised for less torque multiplication and more speed. Should the engine bog, rpm falls off, the flyweights relax their pressure on the flange, and the belt burrows deeper into the pulley groove. This device enables the Peugeot 103 LVS-U3 to climb an 18% grade, yet reach 30 mph on level stretches.

Very little maintenance is required of this and similar transmissions. The main concern is the belt, which must be replaced if it

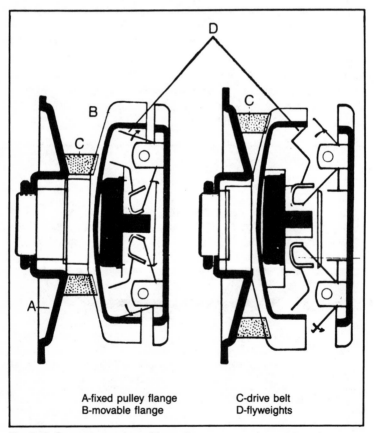

A-fixed pulley flange   C-drive belt
B-movable flange   D-flyweights

Fig. 9-12. Peugeot speed-sensitive pulley.

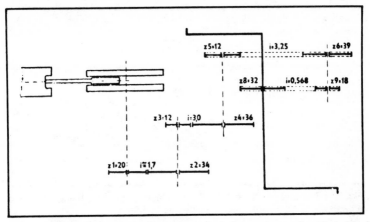

Fig. 9-13. Power flow through the Jawa transmission and rear wheel hub. The numbers represent ratios at each stage.

shows excessive wear or becomes oil-soaked. The flyweight assembly should be coated with high-pressure grease at the pivots and cam ramps.

Gear Drives

Gear drives may be *single-stage* or *multistage*. Single-stage transmissions have one gear pair between the crankshaft and engine sprocket; multistage units have two or more gear pairs in tandem. Figure 9-13 shows power flow through the Jawa Babetta in schematic form. Power leaves the crankshaft by way of a 20-tooth gear meshed with a 34-tooth for a ratio of 1.7 to 1. From there, power passes through a second set of gears, giving an additional reduction of 3 to 1. The overall reduction is 5.1 to 1. Puch gets a similar ratio from a single stage—a tiny engine gear turns a monstrous wheel on the drive side.

Service. Inspect the gear teeth for wear, giving particular attention to evidence of flaking. Sometimes it appears as if the surface metal has peeled, as indeed it has. One problem with moped (and motorcycle) technology is the unwillingness of many manufacturers to use the proper alloys. A very soft gear steel is surface-hardened for a few thousandths of an inch. Once this "skin" is broken, the gear rapidly fails. Normally, the damage is limited to the smaller gear of a pair; however, when one meshed gear gives way, the other must be replaced as well, for used gears do not survive long in the company of new ones.

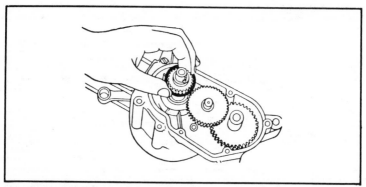

Fig. 9-14. Floating gears can be lifted from their shafts, as is being done here on a Jawa, but watch out for loose needle bearings.

Floating gears—gears that are free to idle—can be removed from their shafts once the bolt or spring clip is undone (Fig. 9-14). These gears may float on uncaged needle bearings, however, and some care must be exercised not to lose any of the needles. Installation is easier if the needles are held with heavy grease or beeswax. Gears that turn with their shafts are held by through-bolts and keys. The shaft/gear fit is deliberately tight and a gear extractor will be needed (Fig. 9-15).

Excessive gear wear is often the fault of the shaft bearings. Bushings should be replaced each time the gear set is disturbed. In many cases, the bushings can be reached from outside the castings and driven inwards with a punch. If the bearing boss is blind, that is, if the shaft does not pass through the case, the bushing can be extracted by either of two methods. One way is to split the

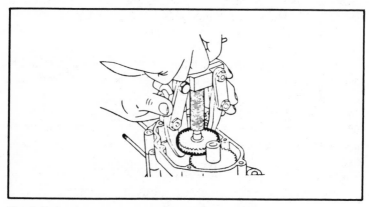

Fig. 9-15. Captive gears must be removed with a puller.

bushing with a small chisel, being scrupulously careful not to damage the boss in the process. Another technique is to fill the bushing cavity with grease, then drive a rod the same diameter as the shaft into the grease-packed bushing cavity. The grease will displace the bushing, lifting it up onto the rod.

Caged needles or ball bearings should not be disturbed unless the wear pattern on the gears shows they have wobbled. These bearings can be driven out of blind bosses by the same hydraulic technique described above, except that the medium is oil-soaked newspaper confetti. It helps if the casting is heated slightly. When installing needle and ball bearings, the numbered side is out, toward the installation tool. Drive the new bearing home with a hardwood block, seating it to its original depth.

Two-Speed Gear Drives

Although three- and four-speed manually shifted mopeds are not unknown in Europe, American laws require that any moped transmission be automatic. The rider cannot be expected to do more than open the throttle. A gear-driven automatic transmission is a fairly complex piece of work, but can give smooth, effortless shifts and is not handicapped by the power losses inherent in belt drive, which can amount to 10% of the input.

Operation. Several mopeds use these transmissions, but all operate on the same theory to give two speeds. At a preset engine speed, one set of drive gears engages, and the other simultaneously disengages. The second, or high-speed, set of gears forms a path for power from the pedals to the engine for starting purposes.

These transmissions have the following parts:

- Two sets of centrifugally engaged clutch shoes
- Two sprag clutches
- Two sets of gears that are constantly in mesh

Figure 9-16 illustrates the driving parts in a Tomas transmission. The bushing (1) supports the two-sided clutch drum (2) on the engine crankshaft. Note that the clutch drum has an integral gear that turns with it: this is the first speed gear. Both sides of the drum house clutch shoes (5), three shoes on each side for a total of six. Two garter springs (12) restrain the shoes. The first-speed shoes pivot on hub 6, which turns with the crankshaft. The second-speed shoes ride on the hub and gear 11. This second-speed assembly floats inside the drum, on the left-handside, as shown in the drawing.

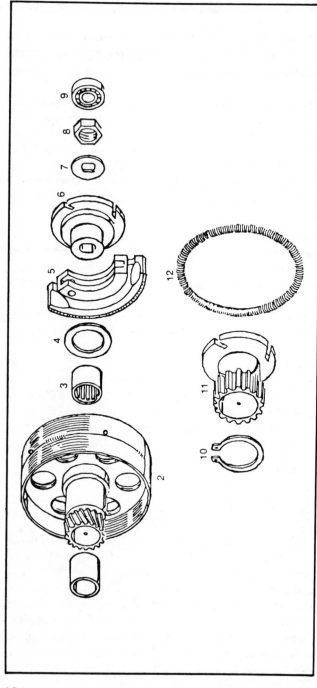

Fig. 9-16. Drive section of the Tomas two-speed, automatically shifted transmission. 1—bushing; 2—clutch drum (double-sided); 3—sprag clutch; 4—spacer; 5—shoe (three on each side of the drum); 6—first-speed hub; 7—lockwasher; 8—nut; 9—bearing; 10—spring clip; 11—second-speed hub and gear; 12—garter spring (one on each shoe set).

The drum can be engaged with the crankshaft by either set of shoes or by the *sprag clutch* (3). Sprag clutches work by means of a wedging action. In the case of clutch 3, the working elements are rectangular in cross-section and held at an angle to the shaft (Fig. 9-17). As this particular example is set up, power can be transmitted from the drum to the crankshaft, but not in the other direction. Once the engine starts, the sprag clutch slips and drum engagement is a function of the shoes.

Figure 9-18 illustrates the driven half of the transmission. The second-speed gear (8) is captive and turns with the countershaft; the first speed gear (6) is mated to the shaft by means of another sprag clutch. Although this clutch is somewhat more complex than the one shown in the previous drawing, it operates on the same principle, allowing power to pass in one direction but not in the other. The first-speed wheel can drive the countershaft, but the countershaft cannot drive the wheel.

Starting. The engine is started by back-pedaling. Power is transmitted by a small starting chain to the clutch drum and, via the sprag clutch under the drum, to the crankshaft. The chain bypasses one set of transmission gears, and so compensates for the reversed pedal rotation.

Idle. The transmission is in neutral, with no power going to the drum (Fig. 9-19A). The sprag clutch slips, because it is biased to disengage when the crankshaft drives the drum and neither shoe assembly turns rapidly enough to engage by centrifugal force.

First Speed. The first-speed shoes turn with the crankshaft. At approximately 1500 rpm the shoes move out against the drum, mating it with the crankshaft (Fig. 9-19B). Power flows through the low-speed gear set where the flow splits. Almost all power leaves

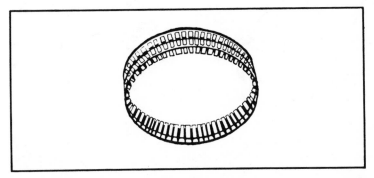

Fig. 9-17. Whatever the form, and there are several, a sprag clutch is biased to pass power in one direction and to slip in the other.

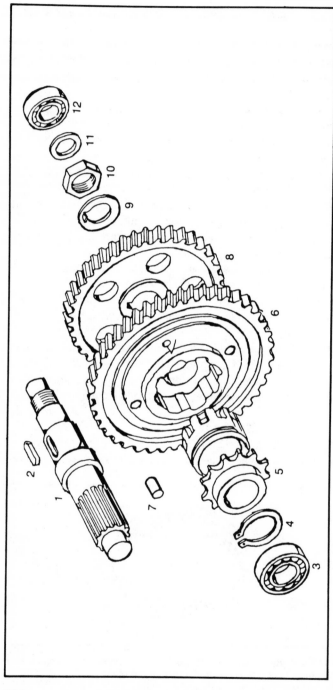

Fig. 9-18. The driven side of the Tomas transmission. 1—countershaft; 2—key; 3—bearing; 4—spring clip; 5—starting chain sprocket and sprag hub; 6—first-speed gear wheel; 7—roller; 8—second-speed gear wheel; 9—lockwasher; 10—nut; 11—spacer; 12—bearing.

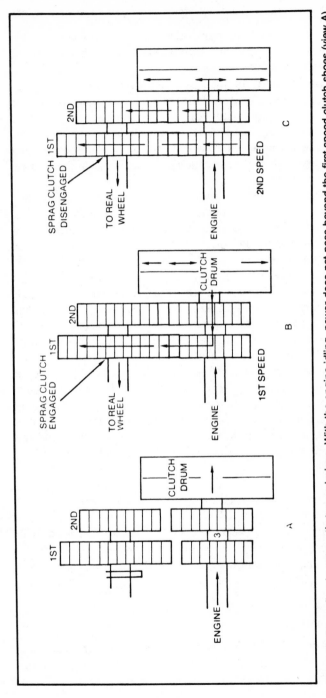

Fig. 9-19. Power flow in automatic transmissions. With the engine idling, power does not pass beyond the first-speed clutch shoes (view A). In first speed, the first-speed shoes contact the drum and power passes through the first-speed gear set and out to the engine sprocket (view B). At five or six mph, the second gear set turns fast enough to engage its shoes; since the countershaft turns faster than the first-speed driven gear, the sprag declutches the gear (view C).

the shaft and goes to the back wheel; a small complement returns to the clutch assembly by way of the second-speed gear set. This power dead-ends at the clutch drum, because second gear is not turning fast enough to engage.

Second Speed. As engine rpm climb, the second-speed shoes reach engagement (Fig. 9-19C). At first glance it would appear that power flows through both gear sets simultaneously, but that overlooks the sprag clutch under the first-speed countershaft gear. Because the second speed gears drive the countershaft faster than the low speed set, the sprag clutch disengages, releasing the first speed set from the drive train.

The sprag between the drum and crankshaft engages only during starting and is rather fragile in comparison with the low-speed sprag clutch. The starting sprag is pressed into the drum and acts directly upon the crankshaft. After a great many starts, the crank may develop waves that interfere with clutch release. Small imperfections can be polished out with emery cloth; deep, fingernail-hanging indentations mean that the crankshaft should be replaced.

The starting sprag should remain undisturbed unless it has failed. In that event, the assembly is driven out of the clutch hub, and a new one pressed into place. The numbered end of the sprag assembly is up, toward the arbor.

Test the transmission before final assembly. Hold the second-speed driven gear—the gear pinned to the countershaft—with your left hand and turn the clutch drum with your right. Both sprag clutches should slip when the drum is turned counterclockwise; turning the drum to the right should rotate the crankshaft and the first-speed gear set. If the transmission does not behave in this fashion, check:

- Clutch shoe/drum clearance. The specification for both shoe sets is 0.4 mm (0.08 in.)
- Interference between the crankshaft nut and the drum. With the nut torqued to 2.5 kgm (18.0 ft-lb), there should be 0.1 mm (0.03 in.) axial play between the drum and shaft. Adjusting washers in various thicknesses are available.

Friction Drive

Velosolex bikes drive through the front wheel by means of a roller that bears against the tire. The engine is mounted in a spring-loaded cradle and lowered into the drive position by a lever (Fig.

9-20). While there are objections to friction drive—accelerated tire wear, slip in rain and mud, the pendulum effect of the engine over the front wheel—the concept is elegantly simple. There is no need for elaborate clutch mechanisms or the complexity associated with single chain drives.

Figure 9-21 illustrates the cradle assembly. Spring tension is regulated by the friction plate and tension nut. The next drawing, Fig. 9-22, shows the centrifugal clutch, drive roller, and their torque specifications.

To remove the centrifugal clutch, undo the nut securing the shoe assembly to the crankshaft. Squeeze the shoes together and withdraw from the drive roller housing. Inspect the linings for wear and replace if necessary. Assemble with the "X" marks on the shoes

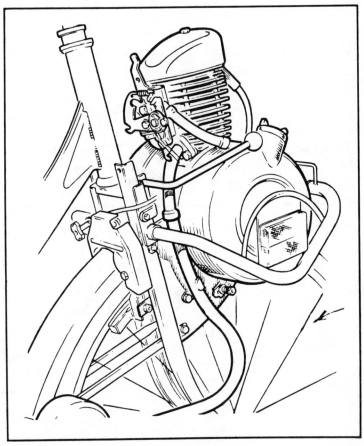

Fig. 9-20. The Velosolex engine mounted in position.

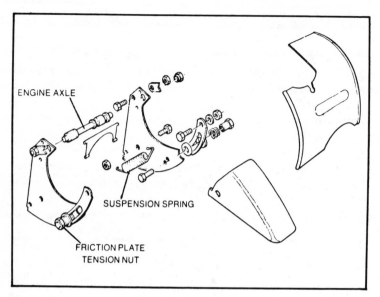

ENGINE AXLE

SUSPENSION SPRING

FRICTION PLATE
TENSION NUT

Fig. 9-21. Engine axle, cradle, and spring assembly. Radical simplicity has always been the Velosolex hallmark.

toward the drive roller. Run up the nut on the crankshaft and mount the wrench shown in Fig. 9-23 over the nut. The arm extending out of the side of the tool should point toward the front of the engine, where you will find an index hole. Bolt the tool down and torque to 65 inch-pounds (about 5.5 foot-pounds).

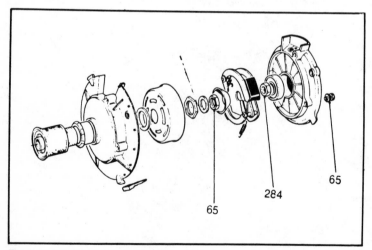

65

284

65

Fig. 9-22. Velosolex drive mechanism with torque specifications in inch-pounds.

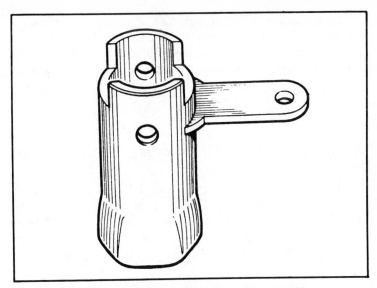

Fig. 9-23. This tool is used to hold the clutch during assembly.

To service the drive roller assembly, gently disengage the seal, deforming it with your fingers. Once it has loosened, work the seal over the crankshaft threads (Fig. 9-24). Install the stroke limiter— the threaded rod shown at the left of the drawing—and undo the drive-roller nut and washer. Remove the drive roller.

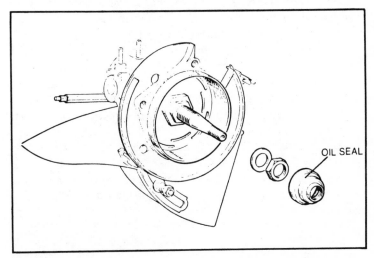

OIL SEAL

Fig. 9-24. Work the oil seal off with your fingers, being careful not to tear it on the crankshaft threads.

201

Lightly grease the roller, confining the grease to the inboard edge where the roller makes rubbing contact with the crankcase flange. Do not get any grease on the friction surface. Align the roller flange with the engine engagement lever bolt hole, and insert a stop bolt. Fit the washer and drive-roller nut and tighten moderately. Replace the oil seal.

PEDAL CRANKS

The pedal crank is arranged to give three options:

- In *neutral* it is disengaged from the engine and rear wheel.
- In *start* it powers the rear wheel and engine.* Should the engine bog under load, the pedal crank can provide additional energy.
- In *drive* the crank diverts all energy to the rear wheel.

How these options are realized depends upon the type of drive mechanism and, to a lesser extent, upon the manufacturer.

Neutral

In the neutral position, the pedal crank is isolated from the rear wheel and engine. On machines with separate drive chains for pedals and engine, a rachet is placed between the rear-wheel pedal sprocket and the drive hub. The rachet, or freewheel, transmits power in one direction—from the sprocket to the wheel hub—and slips when the wheel hub turns faster than the sprocket.

Machines with a single chain to the rear wheel are fitted with a clutch on the pedal shaft. Figure 9-25 illustrates a typical example from Sachs: the driver (5) moves over a thread cast on the pedal shaft in response to friction generated by the brake spring (4). Those who are knowledgeable about coaster brakes will be on familiar ground here. In neutral, the pedals back off against the driver bushing assembly (2). This example has an external arm whose position can be adjusted to suit the rider, thus locating the pedals positively. (On free wheel designs the pedals can be backed off in a full circle and so offer little support for the rider's feet.)

Start

Pedal torque may be sent directly to the engine, or it may enter

---

*Tomas is an exception; the crank must be reversed to start the engine.

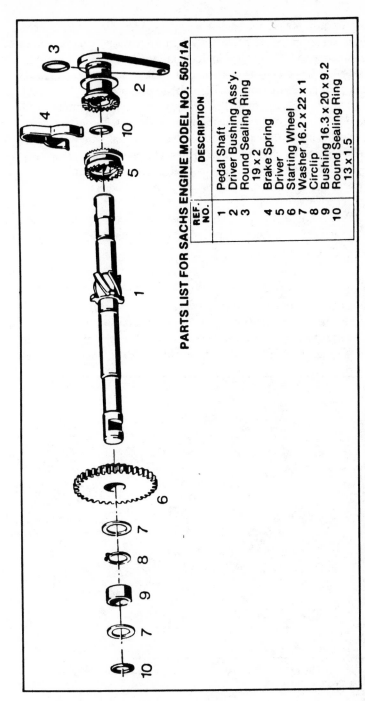

PARTS LIST FOR SACHS ENGINE MODEL NO. 505/1A

REF. NO.	DESCRIPTION
1	Pedal Shaft
2	Driver Bushing Ass'y.
3	Round Sealing Ring 19 x 2
4	Brake Spring
5	Driver
6	Starting Wheel
7	Washer 16.2 x 22 x 1
8	Circlip
9	Bushing 16.3 x 20 x 9.2
10	Round Sealing Ring 13 x 1.5

Fig. 9-25. Sachs pedal clutch. Courtesy Columbia Mfg. Co.

indirectly, by way of the back wheel and engine chain. The indirect approach is limited to bikes with dual drive chains, and is shown in schematic in Fig. 9-13. Single-chain designs route torque from the pedals directly to the engine clutch. Returning to Fig. 9-25 for a moment, note that driver 5 is toothed on both ends. The right-hand end is for positive neutral stop; the left-hand teeth mate with teeth on the inboard side of the gear wheel (6). Torque from this gear splits in two directions: some goes to the rear wheel and some goes to spin the engine clutch drum. The Sachs engine clutch is engaged manually by the same handlebar control that trips the compression release. Other clutches have starting shoes for automatic, speed-sensitive engagement.

Although most manufacturers use gears between the engine clutch and the pedal shaft, a few use a chain. Figure 9-26 illustrates the Morini setup.

Drive

Drive, the condition when forward motion depends solely upon the pedals, means that the engine must be taken out of the circuit. On single-chain machines with manual override on the engine clutch, one does not merely engage the override. With automatic clutches

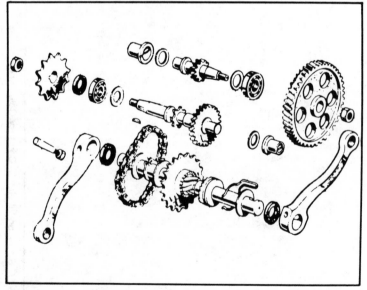

Fig. 9-26. Morini engines employ a short chain between the pedal crank and countershaft.

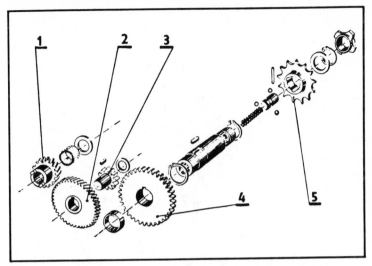

Fig. 9-27. Jawa uses a rather complex collection of parts to lock the engine out of the drive train.

that turn the engine once a preset speed is reached, the uncoupling mechanism is between the clutch and pedal shaft or rear wheel. Figure 9-27 illustrates one form of *lockout*.

Another lockout, typical of belt-drive practice, is shown in Fig. 9-28. The pulley floats on a pair of caged needle bearings (13) on the pedal shaft. It turns with the engine. The pedal crank has its own sprocket, not illustrated here; engine power goes to the back wheel by means of the sprocket assembly 2. The sprocket assembly consists of two toothed wheels; the outboard wheel drives the chain, the inboard wheel can mesh with the lock lever (9 and 15). The lever turns with the pulley and is spring-loaded to hold the pulley in engagement with the sprocket. Turning the engagement lever to the right forces the lock lever out of mesh and breaks the connection between pulley and sprocket. Thus, the pedals can turn without sending power through the rear wheel and back through the engine sprocket and pulley.

Service

The pedals thread into the crank arms. With reference to the rider's seated position, the inboard ends of the pedal axles are stamped "R" and "L". The right pedal has a standard thread, overhand and counterclockwise to loosen; the left one has a left-hand thread. Although the pedals are clearly marked, it is possible

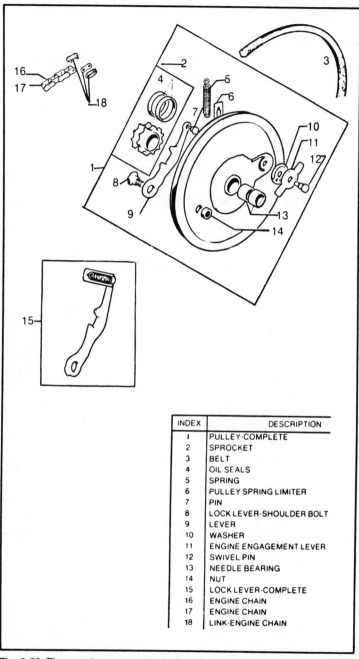

INDEX	DESCRIPTION
1	PULLEY-COMPLETE
2	SPROCKET
3	BELT
4	OIL SEALS
5	SPRING
6	PULLEY SPRING LIMITER
7	PIN
8	LOCK LEVER-SHOULDER BOLT
9	LEVER
10	WASHER
11	ENGINE ENGAGEMENT LEVER
12	SWIVEL PIN
13	NEEDLE BEARING
14	NUT
15	LOCK LEVER-COMPLETE
16	ENGINE CHAIN
17	ENGINE CHAIN
18	LINK-ENGINE CHAIN

Fig. 9-28. The motobecane engine lockout is similar to the mechanism used on other belt-driven machines.

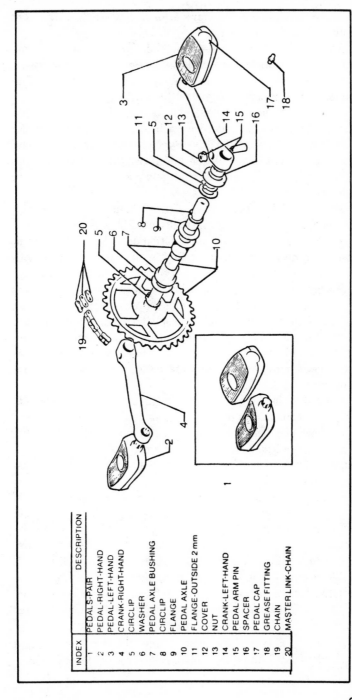

INDEX	DESCRIPTION
1	PEDALS-PAIR
2	PEDAL-RIGHT-HAND
3	PEDAL-LEFT-HAND
4	CRANK-RIGHT-HAND
5	CIRCLIP
6	WASHER
7	PEDAL AXLE BUSHING
8	CIRCLIP
9	FLANGE
10	PEDAL AXLE
11	FLANGE-OUTSIDE 2 mm
12	COVER
13	NUT
14	CRANK-LEFT-HAND
15	PEDAL ARM PIN
16	SPACER
17	PEDAL CAP
18	GREASE FITTING
19	CHAIN
20	MASTER LINK-CHAIN

Fig. 9-29. Motobecane pedal crank assembly. The driven pulley floats between spring clip 5 and 8.

to confuse the right and left crank arms if they are detached from the pedal shaft. Mark them.

As shown back in Fig. 9-26 the pedal arms cross-bolt to the shaft. Undo the nuts, remove the lockwashers, and—supporting the shaft with a wooden block—drive the tapered crossbolts out. The shaft must be supported to protect the bushings.

Relax tension on the chain and work it off the more accessible of the two sprockets. On belt-drive machines, disengage the belt and uncouple the pulley from the drive sprocket. Remove the spring clip (reference No. 5 in Fig. 9-29) and lift off the pulley. Removing the second spring clip (8) frees the shaft and sprocket assembly from the frame hanger.

Most other bikes employ integral pedal shafts extending through the crankcase castings. Further disassembly means that the crankcases must be opened, an operation described in Chapter 8. Polish the exposed portion of the shaft with a strip of emery cloth to remove any rust, then gently tap the shaft out of the casting.

Sliding starter engagement clutches, illustrated earlier in this chapter, are subject to brutal loads. The engagement teeth may round off or the thread may split and splinter. Occasionally, you will find that the friction spring has lost tension. The clue to this condition is erratic clutching—the engine may engage with a few degrees of pedal crank movement, or it may take several revolutions to move the driver.

Pedal-shaft bushings are normally good for the life of the machine, for no one pedals more than he has to. If there is excessive up-and-down play between the bushings and the shaft, suspect that the shaft or the frame has bent. Misaligned engine castings are a thought not to be entertained; if this were to happen, the transmission bearings would go first.

Pedal shaft bushings are available for most bikes and, if necessary, can be ordered through a bearing supply house by dimension (inside and outside diameters and length). Drive the old bushings out with a suitable punch and press the new ones into place. Some distortion is inevitable during installation: correct with an adjustable reamer of the type auto mechanics use. The importance or relative lack of importance of these bushings is underscored by remarks in one manufacturer's service literature. This manufacturer suggests that new bushings be sized with a rat-tail file!

Axial play is critical for some sliding clutches. The standard specification is 0.1 mm (0.025 inch). Adjust the dealer-supplied or bearing-house shims. Lubricate the internals with light grease and assemble.

The Jawa lockout mechanism deserves special attention. The star-shaped part at the extreme left of Fig. 9-27 is known as the control gear, although it is not a gear in the usual sense of the word. It is secured to the shaft by means of the pin. The pin and control gear ride in a slot on the end of the shaft, milled in the form of the letter L. The plunger is grooved around its circumference and slips inside the shaft, where it faces a spring. Engagement occurs between the inside of the sprocket and the three ball bearings. Each bearing is located over a hole in the shaft, one of which is shown.

Turning the control gear counterclockwise allows the plunger to retract so that its groove is under the balls. There is no contact between the balls and sprocket and no power goes to the engine. Moving the control gear in and to the right sends the plunger deeper into the shaft. The groove no longer indexes with the holes, and the balls are forced up into engagement with the sprocket. Power can be transferred from the rear wheel to the engine.

To disassemble, drive out the control-gear pin with a small punch (Fig. 9-30A), extract the plunger (Fig. 9-30B), remove the spring clip and spacer (Fig. 9-30C), lift off the sprocket and, using a copper or aluminum buffer, drive out the countershaft (Fig. 9-30D). Upon assembly, be certain that the balls index with the holes in the shaft and with the groove on the plunger. Once together, the balls cannot escape, and the lockout can be shifted to the "engine on" position.

Engine Chains

Nearly all mopeds use a 1/2 inch by 3/16 inch roller chain for both the engine and the pedals. The first fraction represents the *pitch*, or the distance between the roller centers; the second represents the width of the inner links. Although there is little that can be done about chain pitch, the width of the chain can sometimes be increased for additional durability. The only factor limiting width is the clearance on either side of the sprocket. Wider-than-original chains may foul the spokes or engine case.

Adjustment

Too much chain tension can lead to expensive repairs because the chain, sprockets, and bearings suffer. Too little tension allows

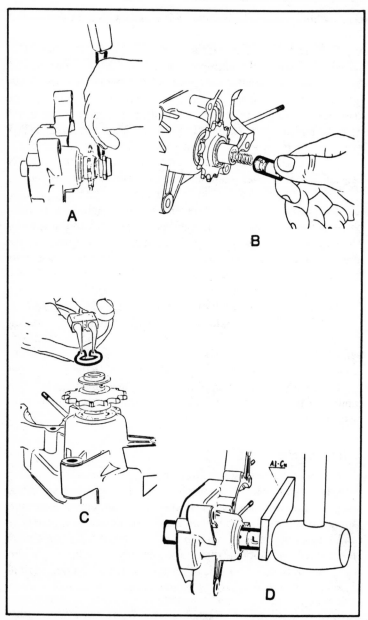

Fig. 9-30. Jawa lockout service. Drive out the control gear pin (view A); extract the plunger (view B); remove the spring clips and sprocket (view C); and tap the countershaft out of the casting (view D). It may be necessary to heat the casting with a propane torch to release the bearing. This technique was described in the previous chapter.

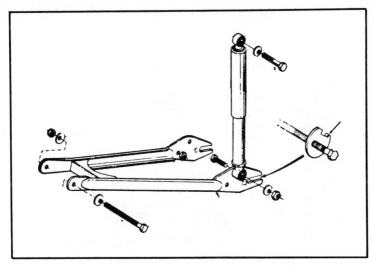

Fig. 9-31. Swing arm, shock, and adjustment cam for the Columbia bike.

the chain to whip and snatch during acceleration and encourages it to jump the sprockets. Adjusted correctly, the chain should have 0.5 inch free upward movement between the sprocket centers. If the bike is equipped with rear spring-shocks, make the measurement with a rider aboard. (The swing arms are never on the same axis as the engine sprocket; weight on the suspension increases chain travel.)

The rear-wheel axle slides in the frame lugs, its position controlled by eye-bolts or cams (Fig. 9-31). Loosen the axle nuts and make the required adjustment. Cams are usually stamped with index marks so that both cams can be adjusted equally. Do not trust these marks to keep the wheel parallel; their value depends upon the trueness of the axle, the precision of the swing-arm bushings, and the integrity of the frame. It is possible to align the cams and have the rear wheel crabbed in the swing arm, a situation that costs power, handling, and tire tread.

A careful owner checks the cam marks against wheel alignment. One way to to this is with parallel boards on either side of the rear wheel. Another, perhaps more accurate, way is to use taut strings. Once the alignment is verified, the cam marks can be corrected and future wheel alignments become almost automatic.

Lubrication

Roller chains are complex, with pins, bushings, and the inside

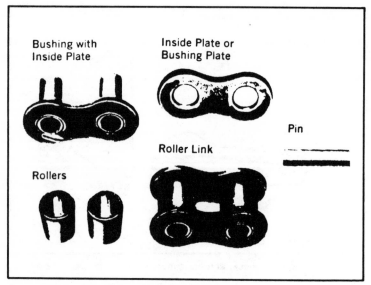

Bushing with
Inside Plate

Inside Plate or
Bushing Plate

Pin

Roller Link

Rollers

Fig. 9-32. Inner-link components. The outer link consists of two side plates, riveted on the pins. Courtesy Daido Corp.

diameter of the rollers masked by other parts (Fig. 9-32). The lubricant must be thin enough to work its way into these parts and, at the same time, tenacious enough to stay on the chain at speed. There are various chain lubes on the market, most of them packaged in aerosol cans and relatively expensive. A more economical alternative is a 50-50 mix of Varsol and 60-weight motor oil, applied with a small paint brush.

The chain should be removed occasionally and soaked in solvent. Moped chains use three-piece master links, easily identified by the spring clip. With a small screwdriver, pry the split ends of the clip apart and push the clip out of engagement with pins. Flex the chain to free the side plate. Once the chain is clean, dip it into a container of lubricant. Allow an hour or so for the excess oil to drain off; then thread the chain over both sprockets. Install the master link from behind, as shown in Fig. 9-33—otherwise the spring clip will not be readily visible. Flex the chain and snap the side plate over the pins. Mount the clip so its closed end is in the direction of travel.

Chain wear is measured by the amount of "stretch", or play between the rollers and bushings. For moderate-duty applications, the allowable stretch is 2%. Because moped chains have an average length of 100 half-inch links, moving the rear wheel back one inch

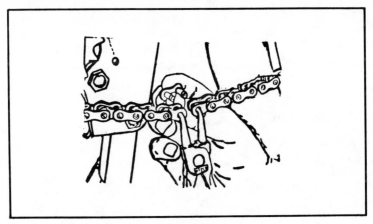

Fig. 9-33. Installing the master link on a Tomas bike.

is the absolute limit. If greater movement is required, the chain should be replaced.

SPROCKETS

The engine sprocket is about one-quarter the diameter of the wheel sprocket and therefore wears about four times faster. Moped engine sprockets are quite small, a tooth or so larger than the 9-tooth minimum that most engineers accept. Even discounting the difference in revolutions per mile, a small sprocket wears more than a large one because of the way it exercises the chain.

The best way to detect sprocket wear is to wrap a new chain over it. There should be some clearance between the teeth and the chain rollers, but not enough to be felt when the chain is tugged. As sprocket wear progresses, the symptoms become more obvious: the teeth appear hooked and eventually wear away.

As a rule, the engine sprocket should be changed as often as the chain. Wheel and pedal sprocket should last the life of the machine.

Chapter 10

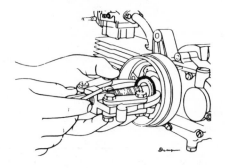

Exhaust System

When the gas-oil mixture in the combustion chamber is ignited, the mixture becomes a vapor and is forced out the manifold through the exhaust system. Stripped to its basics, the exhaust system is a hole in the cylinder that allows the waste vapor to escape.

It that were all there was to the exhaust system, it would indeed be a simple matter to keep clean, and no adjustment would be needed. The noise and power of the gas-oil mix firing creates an annoying racket, however, even in a small, 50-cc. engine, and the exhaust/muffler system was designed to cut down on that noise and reduce power to acceptable and legal levels (Fig. 10-1).

Furthermore, the gases are hot, and some system is needed to carry the hot gases away from the moped and its rider and to help cut down on the force of the discharge.

REMOVAL

The *exhaust tube* is bolted to moped engines, usually on the bottom side. There may be one or two bolts. In either case, make sure the engine and exhaust are cool before working on it. It might take several hours for the exhaust to cool sufficiently after extensive riding (Fig. 10-2).

A short muffler, such as used on the Motobecane, can be bolted to the underside of the engine and clipped near the end. Unhook this clip to remove. Longer mufflers, as on the Puch, have an in-

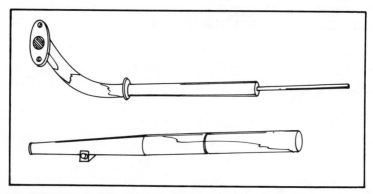

Fig. 10-1. The exhaust system essentially consists of a pipe with a rod on it, an attachment to the engine, and a chromed cover to muffle the sound.

termediate bolt attached to the frame midway along the chromed cover.

Remove the muffler and exhaust by unthreading the bolts to the engine and to the frame if any. There is a gasket between the engine and the exhaust tube. Replace it when you reassemble the exhaust system. On some systems, another gasket (Fig. 10-3) is placed at the forward end of the chromed cover. It also should be checked and replaced if worn.

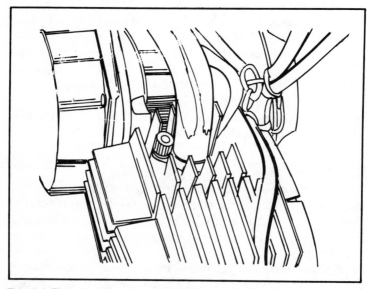

Fig. 10-2. The exhaust attaches to the underside of the engine in the Puch configuration.

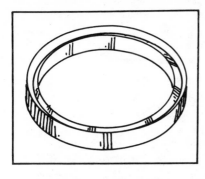

Fig. 10-3. A gasket fitting on the forward end of the chromed cover can cut down on excessive noise if it is in good condition but allows a "putt-putt" sound if it is worn.

In some muffler systems, the exhaust tube is anchored at the rear of the muffler. Remove the set nuts there with a long-nosed plier.

Slide the chromed cover off, and the exhaust tube will be fully exposed.

CLEANING

Carbon buildup will be found all along the exhaust tube and at the exhaust port of the engine. Use a knife to scrape off the worst of the buildup. Commercial carburetor cleaner can be sprayed or daubed on the residue, and the remainder wiped off.

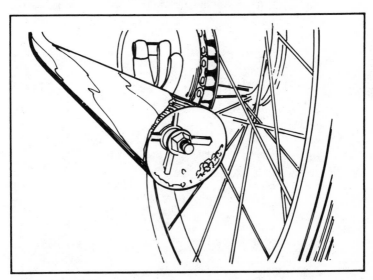

Fig. 10-4. A dirty exhaust, typified by a muffler end packed with old unburned gasoline and accumulated street dirt, can reduce power and efficiency considerably.

The exhaust tube can be best cleaned by soaking it in a cleaning solvent (not gasoline). A long pan or tub is suitable. Use just enough solvent to cover most of the tube. Let it soak long enough (even overnight) to allow the buildup to dissolve.

Don't put the chromed muffler outer tube into the solvent. Use spray cleaner inside it, or place a short length of discarded cable, frayed at one end, into the chuck of a drill motor. Ream the inside of the muffler with that, and then wipe clean with a rag and long rod.

When the exhaust tube is sufficiently soaked, wipe it clean. You might need to scrape heavy amounts of carbon buildup from the neck opening with a knife. Reassemble the unit. On some models, the felt gasket (Fig. 10-3) must be replaced. Check the gasket carefully.

Be sure all the bolts are tightened at the exhaust port and along the length of the system. If the bolts at the exhaust port are loose, it will be no time at all before "putt-putt" sounds tell you they are not tight. In the same way, if the set nuts at the end of the exhaust are not secured, the muffler cover will slide back from the felt gasket and create noise problems.

Smooth travel of exhaust gases through the tube allows more power from the engine. At the same time, the design of moped mufflers forces some of those gases back toward the engine, thus allowing the exhaust system to help maintain the legal maximum speed. Keeping the exhaust system free of excessive buildup permits the

Fig. 10-5. A clean exhaust means better gas mileage and more power.

best combination of allowable speed and power.

The end of the muffler cover can tell you something about the performance of the engine. If the oil is not being fully burned, or the timing is incorrect, wet or damp buildup will be noted on the end of the muffler (Fig. 10-4). Cleaning the exhaust system and correcting engine problems will assure a clean exhaust pipe (Fig. 10-5).

Watch in a rearview mirror for telltale signs of engine wear by smoke coming steadily from the muffler. If the smoke continues, detailed engine work probably is indicated.

Chapter 11

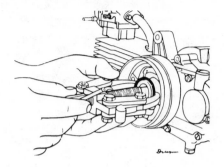

Shock Absorbers

Several years ago, mopeds didn't have shock absorbers or, if they did, they were optional and cost-increasing accessories. As the popularity of mopeds has increased in the United States, however, shock absorbers have become standard equipment on all but the most basic models delivered.

Shock absorbers do just what the name implies. They absorb the jolts of uneven road surfaces and help even out the control of the moped. After any length of time riding on a shock-absorber equipped moped, getting on an old-style bone-cruncher is not a pleasant experience.

Properly speaking, mopeds have only two shock absorbers. These are attached to the rear frame. They are the two tubular pieces connected to the underside of the seat and to the rear swing arm. Most people include the front fork assembly in the category of shock absorbers, however, so I will, too.

FRONT FORK

The front fork is a telescoping assembly connected to the head-frame. In normal conditions it is not necessary to remove the front fork assembly, but once or twice during the life of a moped it is a good idea to doublecheck the front fork. If nothing else, grease inside the unit may need replacement (Fig. 11-1).

To remove the front fork assembly, anchor the moped so that

Fig. 11-1. After taking off the front wheel, drop the front fork assembly from its protective tube.

you are not dependent on the front wheel for stability; it will be removed.

Remove the front wheel by taking off the axle nuts, and the speedometer cable and brake cable. Take off the fender supports.

On the headframe assembly are two bolts (one above each side of the fork assembly). Loosen them and the assembly can be slid down. It will be easier if you remove only one side of the fork at a time. As you lower the fork, be prepared to catch a spring and washer that might slide down quickly.

Unscrew the coil spring from the lower end of the tube and check the lower tube for dirty grease and foreign particles (Fig. 11-2). A multipurpose white grease is sufficient to relubricate the fork. If the grease is dirty, wipe off the tube thoroughly. Don't forget the inside of the outer tube.

Replace the spring, and screw it back into the lower tube. Reverse the disassembly steps to assemble the fork (Fig. 11-3).

If you go over bumps too hard, you could break a plastic sleeve that is on the lower tube in some assemblies. You can purchase the piece separately and replace it; a projecting piece of the sleeve

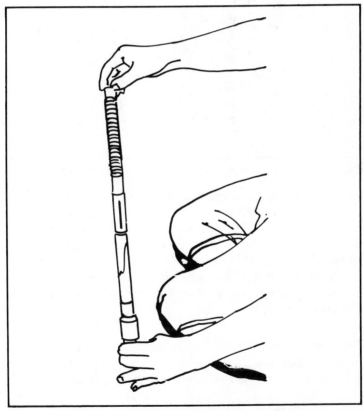

Fig. 11-2. Pull out the spring, check and clean before reassembling.

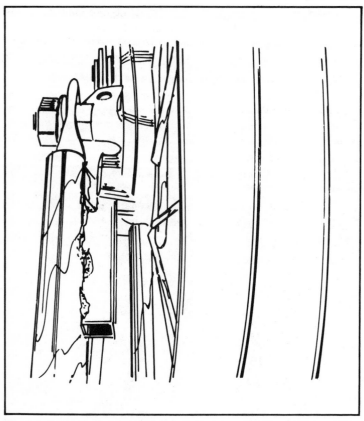
Fig. 11-3. Guide the fork assembly into the notch on the wheel hub assembly.

generally is broken off when the moped encounters a sudden bump or hole. Without the piece, the forks do not handle properly.

Be sure the bolt at the top of the headframe is securely tightened (Fig. 11-4). Then reassemble the fender brackets, brake cable, speedometer cable and wheel.

Be certain the axle nuts are tight. Loose axle nuts can come off, and the wheel can drop off the support arm, causing a serious accident.

REAR SHOCKS

Rear shock absorbers are the main source of cushiony rides, but they are much easier to maintain. Replace them when they go bad.

Replace both at once because the difference in tension between an old and new shock absorber can be enough to throw off your balance.

Shock absorbers are mounted with a bolt at the top, under the seat, and another at the bottom—on the swing arm assembly. Simply loosen and remove the bolts, taking care not to lose washers

Fig. 11-4. Be sure the fork nut is securely tightened.

Fig. 11-5. The rear shock absorbers are easy to take off. Two bolts hold them to the frame.

and spacers attached to the bolts. Insert the new shock absorbers and tighten the bolts (Fig. 11-5).

Chapter 12

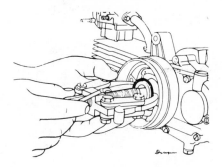

Handlebars, Seat, and Pedals

With a simple machine like a moped, almost every part is vital to proper operation. If a pedal doesn't turn smoothly, it might be difficult to set your feet for correct balance, and you might not be able to turn easily. If your seat is not secured, it might twist and cause you to lose your balance and fall. An improperly aimed headlight can keep you from seeing obstacles at night.

HANDLEBAR ALIGNMENT

Of all those elements that must be correct but which too often are ignored, the handlebar could be the most important. To the careless rider, the handlebar is just a piece of metal tubing attached to the front wheel. You place your hands on it, and it never moves other than to turn the front wheel, so it never should give any trouble. There's more to it than that, however.

Sit on your moped, balancing yourself with your feet on the ground. Now set the front wheel as straight in line with the moped as possible (Fig. 12-1).

Do you get a feeling a symmetry? Does it *feel* like the moped is set up in a straight line? If not, check your handlebars. Chances are they need adjustment; they might be twisted within the headframe, they might not be set at equal distances at both ends from the center of the headset, or they might be set too far forward or back for proper and comfortable riding.

Fig. 12-1. Handlebars should be positioned for easy reach without straining or cramping the arms.

If the handlebars are not properly positioned, you might have the feeling when you are riding that you are constantly steering to one side. One arm might feel extended more than the other. If the bars are set too far forward, you will strain, bent over, and that will make you tired on long rides.

Properly positioned, handlebars hardly are noticed; they feel right. Fortunately, handlebars are easy to adjust. Unfortunately, most riders don't take time to do it right.

Different mopeds have different ways of adjusting the handlebars, but the goal remains the same—line up the handlebars equidistant from the center of the headset and positioned for comfortable riding.

Use the following general guidelines for removing and adjusting the handlebars:

Loosen the screws holding the hand grips and throttle assembly (Fig. 12-2). Do not fully remove the screws.

Remove both hand grips. The cables are long enough to do that without stretching. Lay the grips, with cables attached, to either side of the front wheel, or cross them over the fuel tank. Don't twist or kink the cables.

If the handlebar is to be completely removed, take off the switches (starter switch, light/horn switch, turn-signal switch). Again,

228

don't remove the screw entirely; loosen it enough to slide the switch assembly off the end of the handlebar.

Note: If you want merely to adjust the handlebars, the above steps are not necessary.

Some models have an expander bolt securing the handlebar. This is evident by the large bolt in the center of the handlebar assembly. Loosening that bolt will free the entire assembly, which can then be listed away from the moped. A tap with a hammer or wrench may be necessary to loosen the expander assembly within the stem.

Some models have four bolts and a plate that secures the handlebars directly to the headset or frame. An adjustable wrench, socket wrench, or Allen wrench will be needed to loosen the bolts, depending on the model of the moped. (An Allen bolt has a hexagon-shaped hole in place of the bolt head; the precise size wrench is required, or the bolt can be easily stripped.)

When the bolts are loosened and removed, lift away the handlebar. You may have to twist the bar in the headset and slide it upward.

After a serious fall or an accident, if the handlebars are bent, they should be replaced. It is false economy to attempt to straighten

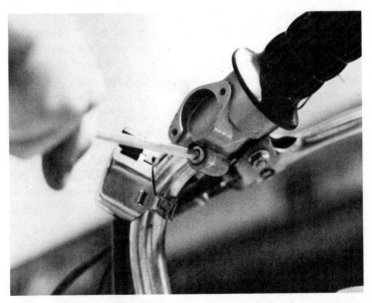

Fig. 12-2. Remove the handlegrips as a preparatory measure to loosening the handlebar.

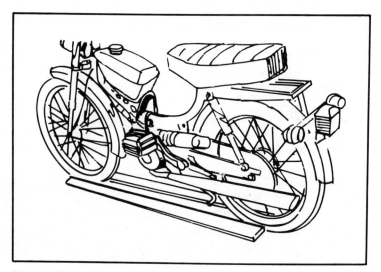

Fig. 12-3. Place the moped between two 2×4s to check front end alignment.

a bent handlebar; replacement is less expensive and easier than trying to regain the correct pitch on a handle. To replace a handlebar
assembly, reverse the above steps.

Any time handlebars have been removed or loosened, they
should be carefully adjusted for the individual rider.

To adjust the handlebars, whether or not they have been replaced, requires an assistant. One-man operations are possible, but
the task of holding the moped upright, positioning the bars, and
then retightening them is almost impossible if you want good results.

Have an assistant do the actual bolt-tightening. The rider should
straddle the seat, steady the bike, and gauge the proper positioning. Never let someone else position the handlebars for you—unless
it's your identical twin. Adjustment is as follows:

Loosen the headset. Center the front wheel in line with the
moped. The more precise you are at this step, the easier the moped
will steer. Place two 2 × 4 pieces of wood against both wheels, assuring they are in line (Fig. 12-3). Tighten the headset firmly. Tighten
the assembly bolt as tightly as possible, short of twisting off the
head; make sure it will *not* slip.

Align the handlebar with the moped. Most quality handlebars
have a crosshatched center. When the bar is properly aligned, the
plate should completely cover the crosshatch. That's a simple way
to center the handlebar. If necessary, measure the distance from the
center of the headset to the end of the handlebars. Tighten the bolts

enough to let the handlebar move slightly.

Sit on the moped with the kickstand up. Have your assistant brace the rear wheel while you balance on the seat and pedals (feet off the ground). Move the handlebar back and forth until you have the correct position for your reach, height, and riding style. Then have the assistant tighten the bolts while you balance the moped. Again, keep those bolts tight. Nothing gives you a more helpless feeling than having the handlebars shift while you are in motion.

SEAT ADJUSTMENT

Proper seat height is as important on a moped as on a bicycle. You must be able to reach the ground with both feet when you come to a stop (Fig. 12-4).

Obviously, the first step in determining correct height comes when you buy the moped. Bicycle-type seats can be adjusted within a fairly great range, but bench-type seats are more limited in range (and a bench-type seat is much preferred for long-distance riding). If the entire moped is too high or too low, seat adjustment probably will not make enough difference for you to ride it safely.

(One man, 6 feet, 5 inches tall, bought a moped and had five accidents on it before he realized that, even with the seat raised to its full extension, he was overbalanced and top heavy. He had to sell the moped.)

Fig. 12-4. Adjust seat height so that your feet are firmly on the ground at stops.

A bicycle type of seat is easily adjustable. A bolt underneath can be loosened and the seat raised or lowered. The seat post will have a mark on it beyond which the post should not be pulled from the frame. Don't exceed that limit; you run the risk of having the seat fall off.

Again, use an assistant to help set the seat height. Put the kickstand up. Set your feet flat or with the heels just off the ground. Sit firmly on the seat. If the seat needs adjustment, step off the moped, adjust the height, and have the assistant tighten the bolt while you steady the moped. Trial-and-error is the method here.

Caution. If you want to raise your heels slightly off the ground when you come to a stop, fine but it calls for greater skill in balancing yourself and the moped, as well as greater skill in starting from a complete stop.

PEDAL ASSEMBLY

All mopeds use the pedal to start the engine at a standstill. If the pedals don't work, the moped doesn't start (Fig. 12-5).

The pedal assembly is nothing more than two rubber-and-metal pedals mounted on the ends of a roughly Z-shaped metal crank. The pedals are secured by a threaded bolt and nut.

Unless you assemble the moped from scratch, the moped's pedal assembly will be complete when you buy it. You should never need to adjust it under normal conditions; just check occasionally that the bolt and nut is not gradually coming loose. If you see threads, simply tighten the nut with an open-end wrench.

Warning: The left and right pedals are threaded differently. You must tighten them in the direction that the pedal normally moves; that is, forward. If you force the nut against the proper threading, you will strip the threads and need a whole new pedal assembly.

The shaft of the moped pedal assembly is a bit more complicated than the shaft of a bicycle assembly, because the pedals drive both a regular chain attached to the rear wheel (to pedal the moped) and a drive chain or drive belt attached to the engine. A lockout device prevents the regular chain from being activated except when the rider turns the pedals and keeps the pedals from turning around at engine speed.

The lockout device, a system of gears, washers, and bearings, allows you to pedal up long steep hills or at low speeds (usually 8 to 10 miles per hour or less) when the rear wheel can't produce enough thrust.

Fig. 12-5. The Motobecane pedal assembly is connected through the drive pulley.

Most pedal shafts are connected through the crankcase (See Chapter 9 for details on removal). Bearings and bushings in the pedal assembly normally are strong enough to last the life of the moped. If your pedals seem to wobble, it might be that the crank is bent or the frame is damaged. That should only happen in an accident or severe fall. If you have fallen, check the pedal assembly for wobble when you go through other repairs.

Chapter 13

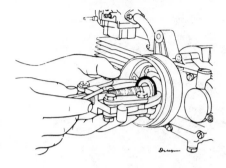

Options

After reading this far, you shouldn't be surprised that mopeds are simple machines. They are economical, trustworthy (with simple care), and a dependable method of urban and even suburban transportation.

There is relatively little to worry about on a standard moped, and the low power means you can't carry much extra weight (although some regularly carry groceries on them and occasionally add a bag or two of lawn fertilizer). There are some options available, however, if you want to use them. They include such things as enclosed throttle grips for cold weather, warning flags waving on a long, flexible pole, and air-powered horns.

The imagination is your only limit as to what may be placed on a moped, although imagination must be tempered with concern for use, weight, and whether the new item will get in the way of careful operation. There are a few "standard options" that many mopedders like to have, however, and we will examine these.

BAGS AND BASKETS

Saddlebags and baskets are the easiest device with which to carry things on a moped. Some people anchor a box on the rear of the luggage spring assembly. That is the least expensive carrier if not the most aesthetic in design.

Wire baskets can be hung (and locked) onto the luggage rack

Fig. 13-1. Enclosed saddlebags can carry a surprising amount of material safe from loss (through bouncing) and from the weather.

assembly. They provide room for a couple of bags of groceries or other bulky items, but the open mesh allows small items to fall through and be lost.

Enclosed saddle bags (Fig. 13-1) do not have the space of an open basket, but they can be secured from the weather, and even locked. They can hold small items without fear of loss. They also present less of a temptation to theft to passersby when you park your moped and leave it.

A windshield is an option that many prefer (Fig. 13-2). Properly attached, a windshield will carry the air up and over the rider's head and yet be low enough to allow the rider to see over it. Mopedders and motorcycle riders should never look through a windshield; always look over the top.

Windshields come in a variety of styles, but all attach to the handlebars. The handlebars should have enough room to accommodate them and switches and controls without interference.

LIGHT SIGNALS

Turn signals are an advantage to a mopedder, who should ride with both hands on the bars at all times. Merely flipping a switch with a thumb allows drivers to see your intention. Most drivers today fail to recognize arm signals because they are not used to seeing them from other cars.

Turn signals also come in a variety of types. You might prefer the simple, battery-operated set used on bicycles, but there are sets

Fig. 13-2. A good and properly installed windshield will push aside most of the wind created by a moped's motion—warmer riding in cold weather.

designed specifically for mopeds and small motorcycles.

The best type has nickel-cadmium (ni-cad) batteries in a sealed pack. The signals are attached through the magneto, so the battery pack is charged whenever the engine is running. The pack can take a considerable charge, but when overcharging is threatened it is necessary to turn on the headlight for a few miles. The pack will drain slightly, even though the battery pack does not operate the headlight. This is a property of the way the turn signals must be hooked into the electrical system. Of course, if you, as most mopedders do, keep your headlights on at all times, overcharging will not be a problem. In fact, if the battery gets too weak, it will be necessary to turn off the headlights for a few miles running to restore a proper charge.

Let your dealer install the turn signals; that's part of his service in selling them to you. Watch what he does so you can repair a loose wire if need be.

Lamps must be replaced occasionally on a turn signal set, and a non-nicad system will require a replacement of standard batteries. This is a simple matter of taking off a cover with a screwdriver, taking out the bad bulb or battery, and replacing it. Make sure you replace with the correct size lamp or battery cell.

Mirrors (Fig. 13-3) are an option no moped should be without. A clear view of the traffic behind you is essential to safe riding.

Fig. 13-3. A long-stemmed rearview mirror is a desirable option for many people.

Fig. 13-4. Helmets are a safety requirement, but the type and variety of helmets and face shields are the option of the rider.

State laws vary on the use of helmets when riding a moped, but they should always be worn by drivers and passengers (Fig. 13-4).

Index

Index